THE PILLAR OF FIRE
AND SELECTED POEMS

Nikolay Gumilyov as a student at Petersburg, 1906 or 1907 (?)

NIKOLAY GUMILYOV

The Pillar of Fire

AND SELECTED POEMS

Translated by Richard McKane
Introduction and Notes by Michael Basker

ANVIL PRESS POETRY
IN ASSOCIATION WITH SURVIVORS' POETRY

Published in 1999
by Anvil Press Poetry Ltd
Neptune House 70 Royal Hill London SE10 8RF
in association with Survivors' Poetry
Diorama Arts Centre 34 Osnaburgh St London NW1 3ND

Translations copyright © Richard McKane 1999
Introduction and notes copyright © Michael Basker 1999

ISBN 0 85646 310 8

This book is published with financial assistance from
The Arts Council of England

A catalogue record for this book
is available from the British Library

The moral rights of Richard McKane and Michael Basker have been asserted
in accordance with the Copyright, Designs and Patents Act 1988

Designed and set in Monotype Fournier by Philip Lewis
Printed and bound in England
by Cromwell Press, Trowbridge, Wiltshire

Acknowledgements

We would like to thank the editors of the magazines *Zenos* and *Modern Poetry in Translation* in which a few of these translations first appeared; and Hearing Eye which published *Poet for Poet*, an anthology of poems, new and selected translations, by Richard McKane in which eight poems appeared. We are grateful to Bloodaxe Books, Newcastle, for permission to include in an appendix six poems from *Anna Akhmatova: Selected Poems* translated by Richard McKane (1989): 'He loved three things', 'I will leave your white house', 'Lullaby', 'Terror rummaging through things in the dark', 'Incantation' and 'Willow'. Helen Szamuely worked with me on some early versions of Gumilyov for readings with the Glasnost Russian Poetry Readers and The Pushkin Club in London. Michael Basker and I are grateful for the scholarship and personal assistance over many years of Sheelagh Graham and the leading Russian Gumilyov scholars: Roman Timenchik, Yuri Zobnin and Nikolay Bogomolov. We would also like to thank Joe Bidder, founder, and Victoria Field, former director of Survivors' Poetry, and Peter Jay of Anvil Press for his meticulous editing.

R. McK.

Contents

Translator's Preface   13
Introduction by Michael Basker   17

from ROMANTIC FLOWERS (1908)

In the Heavens   35
Thoughts   36
Rejection   37
Hyena   38
Jaguar   39
Terror   40
The Lion's Bride   41
The Gardens of my Soul   42
Plague   43
Giraffe   44
Lake Chad   45

from PEARLS (1910)

Barbarians   49
Agamemnon's Warrior   51
Eagle   52
Christ   53
Marquis de Karabas   54
Journey to China   56
Lakes   58
Rendezvous   59
'Do you remember the palace. . .'   60
Kangaroo   61
Parrot   62
Reader of Books   63
'Flowers don't live in my home'   64
This Happened Often   65

Prayer   65
'The palm groves and the aloe thickets'   66
Evening   67
Captains 1   68

from ALIEN SKY (1912)

To a Girl   73
Doubt   74
Fragment   75
Constantinople   76
Modernity   77
Sonnet   78
From a Dragon's Lair   79
I Believed, I Thought   80
Poisoned   81
By the Fire   82
The Ragamuffin   84

from QUIVER (1916)

Venice   87
Conversation   88
Five-Foot Iambics   90
Judith   93
Stanzas   94
Bird   95
Cantos   96
The Sun of the Spirit   98
Mediaeval   99
To Someone Going Away   100
The Sea Again   102
African Night   103
The Advance   104
Chinese Girl   105
Heaven   106
Islam   107
Fable   108

from BONFIRE (1918)

Trees 113
Autumn 114
Childhood 115
The Ice Flow 116
I and You 117
The Peasant 118
The Workman 120
On the North Sea 121
Comfort 123
She Scatters Stars 124
About You 125
Dream 126
Ezbekie 127

from THE PORCELAIN PAVILION (1918)

The Porcelain Pavilion 131
Moon over the Sea 132
'Joyful heart, winged heart' 133
Nature 134
Three Wives of the Mandarin 135
Happiness 136

from TENT (1921)

The Suez Canal 139
The Equatorial Forest 141

from BLUE STAR (1917–18; pub. 1923)

'From a whole bouquet of lilac' 147
'We flew through bright alleys' 148
Shame 149
'Just black velvet...' 150
'The golden night was flying by' 151
'Monotonous, my days flash past' 152
'The soul dozed...' 153
'Your tormenting, miraculous' 154

'My heart had fought for so long'   155
'I said: "Do you want me..."'   156
'A tenderly unprecedented joy'   157
Haiku   157

THE PILLAR OF FIRE (1921)

Memory   161
The Forest   164
The Word   166
The Soul and the Body   167
First Canto   170
Second Canto   171
Imitation of the Persian   172
The Persian Miniature   173
Sixth Sense   175
Baby Elephant   176
The Tram that Lost its Way   177
Olga   180
With the Gypsies   181
The Drunk Dervish   183
The Leopard   184
The Master Craftsmen's Prayer   186
Ring   187
Bird-Girl   189
My Readers   192
Star Terror   194

LATE POEMS (1918–21)

My Hour   203
To ***   205
'The white willow...'   206
A Sentimental Journey   207
The Turkey   211
'No, nothing has changed'   212
'The poet is lazy...'   213
'You and I are bound...'   214
'Don't call the blind music...'   214

'The heart is more aflame. . .'   215
'I played a joke on myself'   216
'I came back'   217

Notes by Michael Basker   219
Instead of an Epilogue: *Some poems by*
    Anna Akhmatova to or about Nikolay Gumilyov   243
Notes to Akhmatova poems by Michael Basker   248

Translator's Preface

Gumilyov was unpublished for sixty years in Russia until *glasnost* in the 1980s. In the West the situation was better with a four-volume Russian edition appearing in the 1960s, edited by Gleb Struve and Boris Filippov. It was this edition that I bought as a student at Oxford and from which I did about 25 translations before and at the time I was working on my first book of translations: *Selected Poems of Anna Akhmatova* (Penguin Books and Oxford University Press, 1969), subsequently published in a new and expanded edition by Bloodaxe Books in 1989.

Time passed, a selection of Gumilyov's poems appeared in the USA translated by Burton Raffel and Alla Burago in 1972, but was virtually un-noticed in the UK, and the grey Gumilyov volumes accompanied me with volumes of Mandelstam on my travels in Turkey and Afghanistan. In an entry from my journal of 13 March 1970 I had written after a telephone conversation with Amanda Haight, the Akhmatova biographer: 'What we are doing or should be is making ourselves into mouthpieces for the poets like Anna Akhmatova, Osip Mandelstam and Nikolay Gumilyov to speak through us. How important this message is can only be judged by future generations. It is up to us to establish the communication. This is the rôle of the translator: to communicate the words of one poet of one country to the readers of the other country. The translator is like a pane of glass through which one can glimpse the heart of the matter, not a mirror or a reflection but a transparent film which should not hold up the eye.' This book of Gumilyov completes the third part of that life's work, but it would have been a very different book without the inspirational collaboration of Michael Basker, who furnished the Introduction and Notes and solved with me many of the problems of translation.

The first poem that attracted me to Gumilyov was 'Agamemnon's Warrior' which I found in Dimitri Obolensky's *Penguin Book of Russian Verse*, that marvellous bilingual collection of poetry, now republished by Indiana University Press as *The Heritage of Russian Verse*, and I well re-member translating it on a ferry from Turkey to Samos in 1966. At that time I was far more a traveller than a poet, or, for that matter, translator.

Gumilyov himself once said that he was a traveller, a soldier and a poet in that order. Travellers and soldiers die, but Gumilyov's poems live on. Gumilyov travelled round Europe, especially Italy and France, with two brief stops in England ('Gumilyov in London' is a video film for Russian TV by my friend the poet, Lydia Grigorieva). But the travels Gumilyov was most famous for were in Africa (or as Voznesensky puns, Girafrica), which he had already visited in his early poems but not in person ('Giraffe', 'Hyena', 'Lake Chad' etc.) On his last trip in Abyssinia in 1913 he gathered valuable ethnographic material for the Petersburg Museum.

Gumilyov was far from a colonialist – he has been widely called the 'Russian Kipling'. The macho aspects of Gumilyov exist in his poetry as well as his life: but I would prefer to call him a survivor. Many of his poems seem to emerge from mental distress. Many of them swing between soaring highs and desperate lows. No doubt it was his poetry, art and travel to Africa that helped him to survive, for it was in the Ezbekie garden in Cairo that he seems to have got over his suicidal impulse. Ten years later, in 1917, he records this pact with himself in the poem 'Ezbekie'. His poetry even survived his own death by a firing squad in August 1921 at the young age of 35, and the death sentence of 60 years' censorship. Now Russians are looking anew at his poetry and sweeping aside the pejorative terms of 'counter-revolutionary, colonialist' that had been levied against him.

Gumilyov loved women (a large proportion of his poems are dedicated to his loves) and after a long and tormented courtship married Anna Akhmatova on 25 April 1910. Akhmatova subsequently said that their long 'engagement' had burnt out their marriage. There are many Gumilyov poems to Akhmatova in this collection – see Michael Basker's notes. The most famous one is 'From a Dragon's Lair'. In later life in the 1960s, Akhmatova was particularly concerned to talk to Amanda Haight, her first biographer, about Gumilyov (to set some of the false information in the Struve-Filippov edition straight) as she had to Pavel Luknitsky. Some of Akhmatova's many poems to and about Gumilyov are collected with notes at the end of the book in 'Instead of an Epilogue'.

When the First World War broke out Gumilyov volunteered and joined a cavalry squadron. He saw active service and was twice decorated with the George Cross. He was a patriot certainly and brave in battle. Throughout his short life he was testing himself.

Akhmatova and Gumilyov had a son, Lev, born in 1912. He was to suffer in the camps for many years for being the son of his parents, and was virtually a hostage to Akhmatova's poetry. He became an expert on Turkic peoples and later a professor at Petersburg (formerly Leningrad) University. He lived to see his father's poetry published again in Russia.

In Gumilyov's poetry death is a constant presence; this sense of being on the edge sharpens his poetry. For some reason he thought he would die at 53 – in fact he died at 35, one of the first writers to die at the hands of the Bolsheviks. He had packed an amazing amount of life into those years and produced by then a corpus of writing that stands with that of the best of Russian poets. This book comes out in the 200th anniversary year of Alexander Pushkin who wrote the famous lines, which Gumilyov fulfilled:

> 'Arise prophet, sense and see,
> fulfil my holy will
> and crossing land and sea
> set aflame with the word the hearts of the people.'

Richard McKane
London, October 1998

Introduction

BY MICHAEL BASKER

In January 1913, the twenty-six-year-old Nikolay Gumilyov published a short manifesto which established him as the effective leader of a new movement in Russian poetry, known as Acmeism. Its date marked almost the exact mid-point of Gumilyov's brief career, which had begun in earnest with a first book of verse in 1905, and would come to a tragic end in August 1921. Its context and principles provide a valuable framework for understanding not only his writing – as poet, critic, dramatist and author of prose fiction – but also the colourful and dedicated life that lay behind.

In the Russia of 1913, the emergence of a new poetic group with a slightly pretentious Hellenistic name would not have seemed especially remarkable, for it coincided with a period of extraordinary cultural ferment and refinement. That same year saw serialization of the first sections both of Russia's most important modernist novel, Andrey Bely's *Petersburg*, and, in an older tradition, of the celebrated autobiographical trilogy by the recently amnestied political exile, Maxim Gorky. In general, though, poetry had by then long superseded the realist prose of the age of Dostoyevsky, Turgenev and Tolstoy, as Russia's most vital literary medium; and Gumilyov's Acmeism came hard on the heels of more stridently self-proclamatory poetic declarations by groups known as 'Ego-Futurists' and 'Cubo-Futurists'. These in turn had followed such short-lived, but intriguing-sounding literary 'isms' as 'Clarism' or 'Mystical Anarchism'. All were substantially indebted to the well-established Russian Symbolist movement, of which Bely was one of the finest representatives.

In the other arts, 1913 was the penultimate season of Diaghilev's *Ballets Russes* – launched in 1909, and danced in Paris, then London, by Anna Pavlova, Tamara Karsavina and Vaclav Nijinsky. The same year brought the première of Stravinsky's *Rite of Spring* (*The Firebird* and *Petrushka* had gone before, in 1910 and 1911). It was the time, too, of Scriabin's musical fame and the first compositions of the young Prokofiev; of Chaliapin's operatic triumph; and the rise to prominence of Russian avant-garde painting – by, amongst others, Larionov, Goncharova and Malevich at home, Kandinsky and Chagall abroad. Acmeism – and Gumilyov's maturity –

were in other words part of the brilliant late florescence of a longer period, roughly contemporaneous with the reign of the last Tsar, Nicholas II (1894–1917), that is now usually termed the 'Silver Age' of Russian culture.

Yet before the beginning of the end of that era was heralded by the outbreak of World War I – to be followed in Russia by Revolution and the protracted horror of a terrible Civil War – differences had already emerged among the six young Acmeists. By early 1914 their movement had lost its initial impetus, and they ceased to function coherently together. The group would therefore have been readily forgotten, as an ephemeral near-irrelevance against the dazzling cultural background, were it not for two related factors: Acmeism engendered three major poets; and in the drastically altered circumstances of later life, all three sought to re-assert their allegiance to Acmeist precepts.

Two of the three, Osip Mandelstam and Gumilyov's first wife, Anna Akhmatova, rank unquestionably among the very greatest poets of a country exceptionally rich in poetic talent, in a century where the extraordinary importance and potential power of poetry became only too keenly felt: as Mandelstam observed to Akhmatova, people lost their lives for it. Mandelstam himself died as a direct result of his writings, in a prison transit camp outside Vladivostok in December 1938. He was 47. Akhmatova, born in 1889, survived until 1966: a figure of immense moral authority, who retained a majestic integrity during long years of persecution, when many of those closest to her were imprisoned or exterminated. The third major Acmeist was Gumilyov himself – executed without trial at the age of only 35, convicted of trivial complicity in an absurdly improbable plot to over-throw the Bolshevik Government. He was the first prominent man of letters to be put to death by the new régime, and a victim not of Stalinism, but of Lenin's 'Red Terror'. His last book of poems, *The Pillar of Fire* – published in the three weeks between his arrest and execution in August 1921, and here translated in its entirety for the first time – was distinguished by a staggering range and intensity of spiritual enquiry, and a new emotional and intellectual profundity. This was matched by the remarkable technical accomplishment of a poet who had been improving not so much steadily as exponentially throughout his career. His achievement at 35 was arguably at least the equal of Akhmatova's at the same age, possibly even of Mandelstam's. As with the greatest nineteenth-century Russian poets – Alexander Pushkin, shot in a duel aged 37, and Mikhail Lermontov, also murdered in a duel at the age of 26 – one can only wonder in awe and regret at what might have been achieved over the next half a life-span.

Before we turn to the short life that was allotted to Gumilyov, however, something more must be said about the 'Acmeism' that seemed to unite these three poets even beyond the grave. (Mandelstam, for instance, wrote to Akhmatova, on the seventh anniversary of Gumilyov's death, of the imaginary dialogue he continued to conduct with those two poets alone, without interruption or foreseeable end. The poems of all three lend compelling weight to his words.) Their movement was conceived in explicit opposition to the long-standing dominance of Russian Symbolism, which, they believed, had lost its way in the fog of its own high-flown metaphysical abstractions. At its simplest, Acmeism has therefore been taken as a 'return to this earth' after the mystical excesses of Symbolism, with an emphasis on precise meaning in place of romantic vagueness and immoderate hyperbole. This has frequently been equated by literary historians with a joyful striving for clarity and simplicity in both form and expression. Yet Gumilyov defined Acmeism 'etymologically', as 'the highest point of something, the flower, or time of florescence', and regarded it as a more well-balanced and mature movement than Symbolism, whose complex legacy he claimed to absorb and develop.

His ambitious intent is partially clarified by the significance which both he and Mandelstam attached in their programmatic formulations to the apparently abstruse and, in a Russian context, initially surprizing subject of the Gothic cathedrals of mediaeval Europe. (A refreshingly tongue-in-cheek example of their outwardly studious enthusiasm is Gumilyov's poem 'Mediaeval'.) As essential background, we should note that, for instance, the foremost Symbolist, Alexander Blok (1880–1921), had often invoked 'cathedrals' as a characteristically atmospheric backdrop to never-entirely-realized meetings with the mysterious, mythologized, 'Beautiful Lady' who is the main object of his poetic quest. With his elusive Ideal in mind – part real, part idiosyncratic (or illusory?) refraction of the Gnostic concept of the 'Divine Sophia' – Blok began one poem, representative of many:

> I love to visit high cathedrals
> With subjugated soul...

For the Acmeist, too, 'high cathedrals' might naturally be a setting for mystical experience (typically, however, an entirely 'realizable' meeting between man and God). But unlike in Blok, Acmeist 'cathedrals' are each *singular*, unique, and endowed with intrinsic value. They might therefore be depicted simultaneously, and as well, as objects of aesthetic splendour; triumphs of architectural technique (sometimes described in the poetry in specific detail); testimony to the dedicated achievement of the anonymous mediaeval masters who constructed them; and symbolic records of the cultural cross-currents which engendered them. Their labyrinthine design might be held to trace the secret wisdom of the Cabala or Esoteric Free-masonry, while the intricacy of each building functions in addition as a metaphor for art: for the essence of the artist's creative and spiritual endeavour, and the ability of his creations to endure through the centuries. The Acmeist approach is in other words emphatically multi-faceted, almost stereoscopic: hence, it could be claimed, more rounded, clear-sighted, and 'mature' than the blinkered, undifferentiatedly one-sided vision of the Symbolist.

To put this another way: whereas the main focus of Symbolism had been the attempt to grasp some 'Higher Reality', Acmeism is 'anthropocentric': its focus is man, and each individual's relation to the 'immediate reality' (or world, or God-given universe) in which he or she finds themself. On a simple level, this is reflected in the psychological, rather than metaphysical, emphasis of Gumilyov's early poetry (e.g. 'Giraffe'), where dreams might disclose the psychological archetypes of a world within rather than a world beyond ('Hyena', 'Jaguar', etc.). From an early stage, too, Gumilyov's poems of exotic lands, distant exploration, and daring adventure convey a (proto-)Acmeistic fascination with the physicality of being, the exhilaration of motion (change, variety), and a striving toward the furthest boundaries of the earth. The early, romantic 'Captains' is perhaps the most famous of these; but again, almost invariably, Gumilyov's voyages are on some level psychological ones of internal discovery (see 'Journey to China'); and as exhilaration gives way increasingly to disenchantment, distant travel becomes a metaphor for spiritual pilgrimage. A related thematic strand — from such poems as 'Lake Chad' to 'Star Terror', from 'Agamemnon's Warrior' and 'Modernity' to the complex personal and historical vision of 'The Peasant' or 'Olga' — involves exploration of modern European man's diminished links with primitive lands and mythological perceptions, and with an (apparently) more psychically vibrant heroic past. Increasingly, too, Gumilyov's poems come to reflect upon the tenuousness of human ties with the animal and more alien, vegetable realms ('The Leopard', 'Child-hood', 'Trees', etc.), and even with inert matter ('Conversation'; more indirectly, 'The Persian Miniature', 'The Word' or 'Ring'). But Acmeism, as we have suggested, sought in theory to encompass *all* facets of earthly experience, and to Gumilyov his sophisticated cultural heritage mattered no less than visceral instinct and primal origin. Indeed — to abstract one of the love poems from its context — the Acmeist poet is acutely aware that 'this happened often and will happen again'; for experience, like language, is at once both common and unique. Personality is rooted in cultural tradition, and where that tradition is not explicitly thematized (though it often is; while the commonality of experience means that the number of original themes is severely limited), a rich pattern of allusion, associative and contrastive, to other individuals, times and places, is woven into the fabric of the poetry as a significant component of Gumilyov's Acmeist artistry and anthropocentrism. In this respect, even a cursory reading confirms that Gumilyov was immersed not merely in Russian culture and history, but also in that of Western Europe, classical, mediaeval, and modern. With time, moreover, he was often drawn beyond, especially to the Persian and Chinese orient, but also to 'marginal' civilizations such as those of Gypsies, Celts — or even his whimsical Venutians ('The heart is more aflame. . .'). Yet his later cultural interests were as much typological as specific. Although his mature viewpoint was primarily Christian and Russian Orthodox, in *The Pillar of Fire*, especially, he used the prism of different religious and philosophical traditions as one approach to the ultimate spiritual questions of self, God and the End which Acmeism naturally recognized as a fundamental part of man's existence, and which the experiences of war and revolutionary communism had rendered particularly acute.

It would of course be possible to say a good deal more about the themes of Acmeist verse, and to write at length about its formal and stylistic characteristics (interesting, for example, is the preference for the extended concrete metaphor, such as one finds in 'Baby Elephant'). But beyond the fact that its anthropocentric poetics is essentially speculative rather than prescriptive, perhaps its most crucial distinguishing feature — which saves Gumilyov's verse from undifferentiatedly omnivorous, descriptive cataloguing of experience — is what might be termed its active ethical impulse. In Gumilyov's case, this meant a conscious endeavour to live life to the full (or to the bitter end), not in the sense of hedonistic self-indulgence, but in a testing to the limits, a pursuit, as his manifesto had it, of the 'line of greatest resistance'. This is perhaps most readily apparent in his poetry of war, while the persistent underlying purpose is the development of will and spirit towards a completeness of self-realization. In the middle years especially, such reliance on human potential often has a Nietzschean tinge (e.g. 'To a Girl'). Later on, it is almost invariably tempered by the sense of service to God, whether conveyed directly, or indirectly through metaphor or the poet's dedication to his art. But two further points should be emphasized. Firstly, 'the full blossoming of all physical and spiritual forces' which Gumilyov proclaimed as an Acmeist goal always remained a challenging ideal rather than a complacent accomplishment. In practice, the poetry often deals instead with the sense of a life wasted and opportunity missed or denied: it treats modern man's feelings of alienation, displacement and incompleteness, and the inner disharmony which results from the conflicting demands of body, soul and over-arching, indefinable self. The frustration of debilitating and humiliating distraction from purpose which runs through the poems of *Blue Star* (albeit in concert with a contrasting, but concealed Masonic theme of self-development) is more common than the fierce concentration of intent apparent in the closing stanzas of 'Five-Foot Iambics', in 'Memory' or 'The Master Craftsmen's Prayer'. Secondly, and most fundamentally, whatever the vicissitudes of life, the 'active, ethical' element of Gumilyov's Acmeism entailed the clear-sighted, courageous acceptance of all the beauty and pain it might bring, rather than any form of other-worldly evasiveness or romantic rejection. The solemn renunciation of suicide in his poem 'Ezbekie' is in this respect a definitive moment, and a crucial prelude to the persistent moral concern with how best to cope with living: 'not to fear and to do what has to be done' ('My Readers'). A similar Acmeist attitude would soon lead Akhmatova and Mandelstam to choose against the 'easy path' of emigration, to remain faithful to their human and cultural values in defiance of the destructive barbarism of what Akhmatova famously termed 'the True Twentieth Century', and, like Gumilyov, to accept at whatever cost their duty as a poet and the responsibilities of the poetic calling.

Nikolay Stepanovich Gumilyov was born on the naval base of Kronstadt, guarding the approach to St Petersburg from the Gulf of Finland, on 3 April 1886. His father was a ship's doctor, and eighteen years older than his wife. Before Nikolay's first birthday he retired from the service on grounds of ill-health, and the Gumilyovs moved the short distance to the outlying Petersburg suburb of Tsarskoye Selo. Although there would be interruptions of several years, and the summer months were regularly spent in seemingly idyllic tranquillity on the modest estates which his father's pension allowed him to acquire in the North Russian countryside, Tsarskoye became the future poet's main home until the Revolution. It is famous both as the site of the magnificent late-baroque Palace, built by Rastrelli for Peter the Great's daughter, the Empress Elizabeth, and for its rich literary associations – primarily with Pushkin, whose verse repeatedly evokes his time of study there at the Imperial Lycée, but also with such illustrious nineteenth-century poets as Vasily Zhukovsky and Fyodor Tyutchev. Yet the small town outside the imperial residence – 'lost', as Gumilyov himself later put it, 'amidst the enormous parks with columns and arches, palaces, pavilions, and swans on its sparkling lakes' – was also in reality a staid, conservative and rather philistine backwater, especially favoured by retired military personnel and impoverished aristocrats. For the young Gumilyov, it was the all-too-familiar and constricting environment in which he grew up and went to school; and though autobiographical material is more often deeply encoded in his poetry than presented directly, his subscription to the traditional 'literary myth' of Tsarskoye Selo was always guarded.

Gumilyov's childhood was largely uneventful. From an early age, his mother (to whom he remained close) seems to have encouraged him to a love of reading, and his father to a love for tales of adventure. Partly because of poor health, he was educated almost entirely at home until the age of 10, when the family moved for a while to St Petersburg, and he was enrolled in the Guryevich Gymnasium (the approximate equivalent of a grammar school). This had a fine reputation and some genuinely enlightened teachers. The young Gumilyov, however, showed little enthusiasm for lessons, apparently preferring to conserve his energies for extra-curricular games of imagination and daring (he organized a secret society of schoolfriends), astronomy (he would write several 'star' poems) and a rapidly widening range of private reading. By the time he was 13, this already included translations of Milton, Coleridge and Ariosto as well as Shakespeare and the Russian poets. He had progressed from writing childish fables to composing a poem 'On the Transformations of Buddha' (these juvenilia are apparently lost); and whatever his attitude to school-work, in 1899 he persuaded his parents to delay the annual family exodus to the country in order to take him to the festivities at Tsarskoye Selo which marked Pushkin's centenary.

The following year brought a more dramatic change of routine. Probably because of the ill-health of Dmitry, Gumilyov's older brother by two years, the family moved to Tiflis (present-day Tbilisi), the capital of Georgia. This was a picturesque and exotic place – with another excellent Russian Gymnasium, where Gumilyov studied more successfully than before. Tiflis stood at the end of the famous Military Highway leading north to Russia through the Caucasus Mountains; and the Caucasus, with its spectacular scenery and wild and hostile tribesmen on the fringes of Empire, had been a favourite setting of Russian Romantic poetry. The tradition naturally left its mark on the verse which Gumilyov now began to produce. He published a solitary, undistinguished poem in a Tiflis newspaper in 1902, but another dozen from the period have survived, inscribed in an album which he presented to one Maria Mikhailovna Marx, 14-year-old daughter of the founder of the city's Russian Theatre. And it should be added that in a city where until November 1901 Iosif Djugashvili (alias Koba, afterwards alias Stalin) had taken the lead in fomenting social unrest, Gumilyov also underwent a brief enthusiasm for a different Marx. This incurred the fleeting wrath of the local authorities during the family's summer retreat in 1903, when he attempted to disseminate propaganda among mill-workers and other residents of Ryazan Province. He was hurriedly taken away by his mother.

Politics were in any case definitively eclipsed by new interests and encounters following the family's return north, to Tsarskoye Selo, in autumn 1903. Here Gumilyov discovered Nietzsche and the Symbolists — and became increasingly convinced of his own vocation. A more personal influence was Innokenty Annensky, the headmaster of his new school, the Tsarskoye Selo Boys' Gymnasium, who happened also to be an innovative and intellectually refined decadent poet: first-rate but then little recognized, and somewhat apart from the Symbolist mainstream. Gumilyov (who again made poor academic progress: he had to repeat a year because of failure in mathematics, and did not leave school until he was 20) moved gradually under his poetic and ideological sway. The slow rapprochement continued after the Gymnasium, until Annensky's sudden death from a heart attack in 1909. Gumilyov was justified in subsequently proclaiming him an inspirational precursor of the Acmeists.

Another encounter in Tsarskoye Selo at the end of 1903 had a still greater impact. This was a first meeting with the 14-year-old schoolgirl, Anna Andreyevna Gorenko — who later assumed the pen-name of Akhmatova. By the following May, Gumilyov had solemnly declared his love; and by the time Gorenko-Akhmatova was taken to Kiev by her mother after her parents' separation in summer 1905, he had at least twice proposed marriage (or lengthy engagement), and twice been turned down. The relationship was broken off before Akhmatova's departure, but Gumilyov maintained indirect contact by befriending and corresponding with her brother Andrey. This set a pattern for the protracted courtship (or non-courtship) which lasted until the couple finally married, to the unanimous disapproval of Akhmatova's relatives, in April 1910.

Despite long separations and Gumilyov's occasional pursuit of other women (then as throughout his life, almost always both strikingly beautiful and considerably younger than him), he was passionate, steadfastly importunate, and driven to such despair by Akhmatova's seeming indifference, bemusement, and avowed liaison with an older man, that he more than once attempted suicide. Yet she was capable, too, of tempestuous scenes, cruel taunts, and deliberate torment; on occasions herself re-instigated communication with Gumilyov; and eventually chose to accept him – albeit, perhaps, more from a mixture of respect and compassion at his sheer persistency than unhesitating love. According to Akhmatova's childhood friend, Valeriya Sreznevskaya, the entire relationship constituted a kind of 'secret duelling': 'on her part, for self-assertion as a free woman, on his, from a desire not to surrender to any sorceress's spell, but to remain himself, independent and powerfully self-possessed. . .'. Not surprisingly, the marriage which ensued was happy only for a short time. On the level of everyday life (in which neither partner was particularly skilled) they soon drifted apart. Each embarked on a series of other sexual involvements, and the divorce which Akhmatova requested in August 1918, though painful to Gumilyov, was merely the formal acknowledgement of a long-standing separateness. On another level, however – of poetry and spiritual concerns, or as Sreznevskaya put it, 'some kind of rarefied heights not accessible to ordinary mortals' – they remained unerringly close, and the poetic dialogue between the two is more extensive on both sides than has hitherto been acknowledged. The image of Akhmatova haunted Gumilyov's writing throughout his career; and there may be truth, too, in her later opinion that his near-compulsive 'Don-Juanism' (or what she called his amatory 'stake on quantity'), and even his distant travels, resulted from the failure of his single love, the 'Damayanti' he sought and lost ('Five-Foot Iambics').

The various encounters which followed Gumilyov's return to Tsarskoye in 1903 bore fruit in a first book of verse, *Path of Conquistadors*, published at his own expense in October 1905. The poems show not the slightest trace of that year's political upheavals, but often reflect the image of Akhmatova, and are immoderately and indiscriminately imitative of Russian Symbolism. The principal models were Bely and Konstantin Balmont, but there were echoes, too, of Blok and others, with an ill-assimilated admixture of Lermontov and Pushkin. Gumilyov nevertheless took the step of sending a copy to Valery Bryusov, another prominent Symbolist writer, and editor of the most important Symbolist journal, *The Scales*. A brief and appropriately lukewarm review duly appeared there. More importantly, it was followed, three months later, by a letter from Bryusov which initiated a sometimes intensive correspondence lasting several years. In effect, Gumilyov had been severely chastened by Bryusov's judicious assessment of his premature début (which he long sought to consign to oblivion). With typical resolve, he had nevertheless determined to persevere, in order to transform himself into a truly accomplished and original poet: not however by striving to avoid any further influence, but through a lengthy period of dedicated 'apprenticeship' to more consciously selected and congenial 'masters of the pen'. Bryusov, a great proselytizer, temperamentally similar to Gumilyov, proved himself the ideal mentor. His imprint was strongly apparent in his willing pupil's next volume, *Romantic Flowers* (published, again at his own expense, in 1908) and, to a lesser degree, in *Pearls*, brought out by Bryusov's prestigious Scorpio publishing house in 1910. Yet Gumilyov persisted, too, with isolated experiments in the manner of other older contemporaries; and as he progressed, with remarkable facility, from imitation to creative assimilation and occasional parody of his Symbolist sources, his range of literary and cultural reference broadened immensely. In *Pearls* and his next book, *Alien Sky* (1912), this can be seen in the emergence of an enduring penchant for fresh exploitation of archetypal literary themes, and for corresponding 'conservative innovation' in the handling of formal traditions. The conscious 'literariness' of Acmeism, and its values of self-discipline and craftsmanship, are thus profoundly rooted in Gumilyov's early poetic practice.

In 1906, however, his Acmeistic stoicism was still not fully developed. For reasons probably connected both with rejection by Akhmatova and regret over his first book, he chose to begin his serious apprenticeship by abandoning Russia. That autumn he left for Paris – with little money, and against his parents' inclination – on the pretext of study at the Sorbonne. He seems to have been far from assiduous in attending lectures on Art and Mediaeval French Literature, but evidently read voraciously, and worked hard at his writing. On the advice of Bryusov, this now included several short stories (on exotic themes, with autobiographical subtexts). Gumilyov also endeavoured to widen his circle of literary acquaintances among the many Russian intellectuals who frequented the French capital. Unfortunately, the most prominent of these – Dmitry Merezhkovsky and his wife Zinaida Gippius – were devastatingly unencouraging. Gippius acerbically described Gumilyov as a sententious, putrescent and dismally ignorant youth, who 'sniffed ether' (drugs did indeed figure at several points in his career) and claimed Jesus and Buddha as mere precursors. He encountered a rebuff, witnessed by Andrey Bely, which he resented for the rest of his life. Younger acquaintances, French as well as Russian, were more amenable, and Gumilyov and two Russian associates even produced a short-lived literary and artistic periodical, *Sirius*, in which Akhmatova made her poetic début. The overriding impression of his 'Parisian period' is nevertheless of his deep solitude and depression. His misery was probably little alleviated by a theoretical and practical study of occultism, which included a necromantic attempt to summon the Devil. (He was horrified when, after fasting and other ritual preparation, a vague figure did indeed begin to take shape in his room). It can be detected, too, behind a restlessness which once led to his arrest for vagrancy in Normandy (possibly in the aftermath of attempted suicide), and found expression in somewhat furtive and uncomfortable journeys to Southern Russia for unrewarding meetings with Akhmatova.

Against this background, literary progress may have seemed success against the odds. With Bryusov's help, Gumilyov nevertheless began gradually to publish in several prominent periodicals, and the older poet's generally favourable reaction to *Romantic Flowers* gave him the confidence to return to Russia in spring 1908. From his home in Tsarskoye, he now sought active involvement in Petersburg literary life, and his continuing determination to analyse and master the secrets of his craft found a new outlet in published reviews of recent books of verse. From his association the following year with Sergey Makovsky's prestigious new journal *Apollo* — which soon became a forum for Acmeistic opposition to Symbolism — his regular 'Letters on Russian Poetry' evolved into authoritative models of succinct, elegantly formulated, well-motivated and perceptive literary judgement. Even in 1909, however, he was still as anxious to learn as to evaluate and teach. His recurrent, despondent sense of a hiatus in his development led him to instigate a series of seminars on poetry under the initial guidance of Vyacheslav Ivanov, the formidably erudite Petersburg Symbolist (Bryusov was a Muscovite), whose famous bohemian-intellectual 'Tower' he began to frequent. This proved the final catalyst to Gumilyov's creative emancipation. By April 1911, his differences with the older poet had become irreconcilable, and his poem-cycle on the 'Prodigal Son' effectively led each to discern in the other an irredeemable blasphemy. Ivanov's hostility prompted Gumilyov and other young colleagues to establish an alternative 'Guild of Poets'. The name signified, in part, a shift from Symbolist 'theurgy' to spiritual restraint and formal craftsmanship; and Gumilyov himself now assumed the rôle of guiding spirit and literary arbiter, of 'maître' rather than pupil-apprentice. Polemical debates over the current condition of Russian poetry ensued, and by late 1912 Gumilyov, together with Akhmatova, Mandelstam and three other Guild members, was ready to announce the advent of Acmeism.

Akhmatova later regarded the still young Gumilyov's opposition to Ivanov's redoubtable personal and intellectual authority as an act of 'civic courage'. As he gradually established his own reputation, however, he also courted other, less metaphorical forms of danger. A notorious example was his duel in November 1909 with the poet Maximilian Voloshin. The tangled pretext was the improbable creation of a fictional Catholic poetess (one Cherubina de Gabriak) by Voloshin and Elizaveta Dmitriyeva, who had switched her affections that summer from Gumilyov to Voloshin. The highly-charged literariness of the proceedings was emphasized by the choice of venue – Chyornaya Rechka, where Pushkin had once confronted D'Anthès, and Lermontov de Barante – and neither combatant was hurt. Predictably, the spectacle of two 'decadent' poets fighting with pistols at the beginning of the 20th century caused considerable mirth in the press, and little consternation to the authorities, who fined the participants 10 roubles apiece. Yet the outcome might have been tragic, had Voloshin's second not surreptitiously tampered with his gun, which twice misfired. (Gumilyov protested in vain that Voloshin should be allowed another shot.) Ultimately, the absurd episode probably strengthened Gumilyov's resolve to free himself of the 'demonic' freneticism of the Symbolist milieu.

Certainly in the coming years Gumilyov showed himself ready to abandon the literary scene (and perhaps, too, the emotional complexities of domestic life) for protracted periods. At the end of 1909 he left on a four-month journey to Abyssinia, but failed to reach the capital. In autumn 1910, only four months after honeymooning in Paris, he accordingly abandoned his wife for a longer, six-month expedition. This time he went via Constantinople, Port Said and the Nile, and reached Addis Ababa inland through desert and mountains from Djibouti. Though he and Akhmatova toured Italy together in 1912, it therefore seems unsurprising that in 1911 Akhmatova should have gone alone to Paris – leaving her husband behind to flirt with his distant cousin Olga Kuzmina-Karavayeva, and fall seriously but platonically for her sister Masha, at his mother's newly inherited country home of Slepnyovo.

Gumilyov approached Africa with a remarkably open mind. Though inevitably conditioned by the attitudes of his age, he showed little of the white-imperialist prejudice of which Soviet detractors would ritually accuse him. His first, hazardous trip was by mule train through Dire Dawa to Harer. With his skin burnt and his clothes in tatters, he felt that he was simultaneously living two dreams: 'one unpleasant and arduous to the body, the other ravishing to the eye'. He returned intoxicated by the experience, with the hides of the several animals he had hunted. The next year he befriended Abyssinian poets and artists, met Emperor Menelik – ruler, as Gumilyov emphasized, of the largest independent country in Africa – and collected folk songs, paintings and everyday utensils. He returned with tropical fever and an apparent disenchantment with travel. But in spring 1913 – only four months after the inception of Acmeism, and seven since the birth of his son Lev – he nevertheless left once more for Abyssinia and the Somali Peninsula. He was away again for half a year, his ethnographical aspirations this time officially (though modestly) financed by the Academy of Sciences. He and his nephew Kolya Sverchkov brought back a rich and varied collection – long proscribed, like Gumilyov's writings, but now housed in the St Petersburg Museum of Anthropology and Ethnography. There is also a fascinating photographic record of their expedition. Gumilyov afterwards dreamed of visiting Madagascar; and his continued, unrealizable, nostalgic yearning for Africa was poignantly registered in such late poems as 'A Sentimental Journey'.

It is easy to appreciate that by comparison with meeting the future Haile Selassie, crossing the crocodile-infested Webbe, or enduring a summer heat too intense for travel by day, everyday literary life in Petersburg should have seemed flat. Gumilyov wrote little new poetry in late 1913 or the first half of 1914, concentrating instead on literary criticism and verse translation (principally from Gautier and Robert Browning). His mood doubtless contributed to the internal Acmeist dissension referred to above, and helps to explain an unconcealed enthusiasm at the outbreak of World War I, which might now seem morally repugnant. Alone among established writers, Gumilyov at once volunteered for military service. It seems clear, however, that he was motivated not by chauvinist bigotry, but primarily by that same striving for inner development which had already impelled him toward both Africa and Acmeism. He enlisted in the cavalry as an ordinary soldier; and his fundamentally ascetic pursuit of spiritual discipline and physical ordeal acquired invigorating vindication from a sense of oneness with the Russian people. Like the deepening Orthodox faith which seemed naturally to underpin his outlook, this tended perpetually and tormentingly to elude most of the country's cultural élite, and signified a further departure from his previous Symbolist milieu.

Gumilyov was in uniform until late spring 1918 and saw considerable action on the Eastern Front, in present-day Poland, Lithuania and Latvia. (There were also long spells in hospital and convalescent homes, due to illness ultimately attributable to his African exploits.) He fought with predictable courage, and distinguished himself by his skill and daring with small, free-ranging cavalry units conducting reconnaissance or guerrilla-like operations. He was decorated three times (twice with the George Cross), and documented his experiences in prose. But as the war became literally entrenched, with machine-gun and heavy-artillery fire on the ground and the first military aeroplanes overhead, Gumilyov's preference for the cavalry was patently anachronistic, and he again suffered acute disillusion. (Its most eloquent expression is his finest verse drama, *Gondla*, which also reflected his affair with the future 'revolutionary heroine' Larisa Reisner.) He prepared for but failed his officers' exams (because of his poor mathematics), and when his Hussar Regiment was partially disbanded in early 1917, tried instead to alter his circumstances by applying for transfer to the Russian Expeditionary Corps. Some months after the February Revolution (which he witnessed with equanimity) he was duly dispatched to the Salonican Front – but never reached it. He set sail via Sweden to London, where he spent the last two weeks of June 1917. There, amongst others, Gumilyov met through Boris Anrep (the mosaicist and close friend of Akhmatova) such luminaries as Roger Fry, Chesterton, Yeats (fleetingly) and Aldous Huxley, and attended one of Lady Ottoline Morrell's weekend gatherings at Garsington Manor. But the next stage of his journey took him no further than Paris. He remained there through the rest of 1917, serving, in effect, as indispensable administrative assistant to the Military Commissar of the Provisional Government, General Rapp.

In Paris once more, Gumilyov spent much time with the Russian artists Larionov and Goncharova – and collaborated with both on separate ballet libretti for Sergey Diaghilev. One of these gave rise to his 'Byzantine' play *The Poisoned Tunic*. He also paid persistent court to a certain Yelena Dubouchet, whose resistance is recorded in his posthumously published *Blue Star* cycle. Gumilyov's military duties, which included maintenance of order among Russian troops in France, were nevertheless complex and taxing. In particular, he was involved as negotiator in protracted dealings with rebellious troops encamped at La Courtine, near Limoges. The mutiny was eventually suppressed by force, and Gumilyov was left to compile an investigative report. He found the episode traumatic, and, in view of the rôle played by Leninist-Anarchist propaganda, a profoundly dispiriting omen for the future of Russia.

In January 1918 the former Provisional Government's military jurisdiction in France was curtailed, and Gumilyov returned to London, hoping to reach the Mesopotamian Front. When this proved impossible, he worked for a while at India House, in the Ciphers Department of the Russian Government Committee; planned (or continued) a first novel and a book on *The Theory of Integral Poetics*; and possibly became involved with the daughter of the former Russian Ambassador. By April all funds for his maintenance were exhausted, and he was ordered home to Russia.

Back in Revolutionary Petrograd (as the city had been renamed when War broke out) Gumilyov threw himself into literary life with an unprecedented and henceforth unabating enthusiasm, evidently attributable more to invigoration after long absence than to the sheer necessity of working ever harder to support a family through the desperate deprivations of (Civil) War Communism. (He hurriedly married Balmont's step-daughter, Anna Engelhardt, after his divorce from Akhmatova in summer 1918, and she bore him a daughter, Yelena, in April 1919. But by November material conditions were so bad that the family was dispatched to Gumilyov's mother in Tver Province, and they lived apart until May 1921.) To begin with, Gumilyov embarked on an ambitious scheme of publication which began with his sixth book of original verse, *Bonfire*, an 'African' narrative poem, and his versions of oriental poetry in *The Porcelain Pavilion*. He was commissioned to write the African cycle of *Tent*, and published his translation of *The Epic of Gilgamesh*, which he had been working on for some time with the Assyriologist, and Akhmatova's second husband, Vladimir Shileyko.

But by early 1919, the acute paper shortage forced him to channel his energies elsewhere. He spent a great deal of time over the remaining years editing and translating for Gorky's projected 'World Literature' series. Gumilyov's translations included poems by Coleridge (an excellent *Ancient Mariner*), Southey, Blake, Wordsworth, Tennyson, Swinburne, Heine, Leopardi, Rimbaud, Baudelaire, Voltaire – and many, many others. The list of edited translations and introductions is more extensive still. In addition to this, Gumilyov taught the theory, history and practice of poetry, often lecturing several times a week, and otherwise devoting considerable attention to a coterie of younger writers. He seemed indefatigable, too, as a prominent member of numerous literary-cultural committees which were then vital to the very physical survival of the intellectual community; and in 1921 he was elected Chairman of the Petrograd Branch of the Russian Union of Poets. Though it is difficult to see how he found time for original work (let alone alleged political conspiracy), he produced much new drama; the tantalizingly impressive first cantos of a narrative *Poem of the Beginning*; a crop of sometimes experimental lyrics; and above all, the splendid poetry that would make up *The Pillar of Fire*. There was no doubt that he was arrested at the height of his powers, full of fresh creative plans.

To judge by the surviving record of interrogation, Gumilyov's most serious crime was an admission that, had the Kronstadt revolt of March 1921 spread to Petrograd, he would have been prepared to fight on the side of the insurrectionists. His 'guilt' was otherwise attested only by the comparably flimsy allegations of one, or perhaps two, shadowy *agents provocateurs*. But his arrest probably coincided with a wave of terror directed specifically against intellectuals, and he was doomed in advance. On 24 August 1921, he was sentenced to death.

Gumilyov was shot together with 60 other so-called 'Tagantsev conspirators'. In accordance with established practice, the executions took place in a forest outside Petrograd, probably in the early morning of 25 August. The bodies were consigned to an unmarked, communal grave. By 1923 Gumilyov's works were proscribed in Russia, and those close to him began to suffer. Lev, his son by Akhmatova, and later an outstanding historian, ethnographer and cultural philosopher, was repeatedly arrested because of his parentage, and spent a full decade in the camps. (Gumilyov's second wife and daughter, however, died of cold and hunger in 1942 during the Siege of Leningrad.) Yet his poetry continued to be read clandestinely, and was studied and reprinted in the West. And coincidentally with the centenary of Gumilyov's birth in 1986, cautious re-publication of his poetry at home became one of the first signals of Gorbachev's policy of *glasnost*. Publication figures since then clearly suggest that he is now one of Russia's most popular poets.

Bristol, October 1998

From *Romantic Flowers*

These days flared brighter than gold
and the Great Bear-night ran.
Catch her, prince, catch her,
lasso her and strap her to your saddle!

Lasso her and strap her to your saddle,
and then in the pale blue tower
show the Great Bear-night
to your knightly Dog.

The Dog holds on with deadly grip,
he is brave, powerful and cunning,
he has been bearing a beastly anger
for bears from time immemorial.

There is no escape for her anywhere
and she breathes her last,
so that Capricorn, Aries and Taurus
can safely graze in the sky.

Why do thoughts gather in on me,
like thieves by night in the silent murk of the suburbs?
Like vultures, malevolent and gloomy,
why do they demand cruel revenge?

Hope went away and dreams ran off,
my eyes opened from stress
and I read on a ghostly tablet
my words, deeds and musings.

Since I, with calm eyes,
looked at those sailing away to victories,
since I, with burning lips,
touched lips that knew no sin,

since these hands, these fingers
did not know the plough, were too slender,
since songs, eternal wanderers,
only wore me down, sorrowful and ringing,

now the time of revenge has come for all this.
Blind men will destroy the fraudulent, tender temple,
and thoughts, thieves in the silence of suburbs,
will suffocate me in the darkness like a beggar.

Empress, or maybe just a sad child,
leaned over the sleepily sighing sea,
and her fine sinuous figure seemed so slender,
rushing secretly into the silver dawns.

Twilight vanishing. Cry of a bird,
the dolphins flashed before her through the sea.
They'll swim to the turquoise kingdom
of the lovelorn prince – they offer their polished backs.

But the crystal voice sounded emphatically clear
as it stubbornly spoke the fateful 'No. . .'
Empress or maybe just a wilful child,
a tired child with helpless torment in her eyes.

By the reeds of the languid Nile
where only butterflies and birds fly,
lies hidden the forgotten grave
of a wicked but enchanting empress.

The dark night bears its illusions.
The moon rises like a sinful siren,
whitish mists swirl around
and a hyena steals from a cave.

Its wailing is furious and foul,
its eyes evil and doleful,
its menacing teeth fearsome
over the roseate marble of the grave.

'Look moon, lover of the mad,
look stars, slender apparitions,
and dark Nile, ruler of noiseless waters,
and butterflies, birds and plants.

Let everyone look at my fur standing on end,
my eyes blazing with evil sparks.
Am I not an Empress too,
like she who sleeps beneath the stones?

Her heart beat, full of treachery,
her arched brows carried death.
She too was a hyena,
like me she loved the smell of blood.'

Dogs wail in terror in the villages,
small children cry in their homes.
The sullen fellahin reach for
their long, merciless lashes.

I had a strange dream last night:
I dreamed that I was gleaming in the sky,
but that life, a monstrous procuress,
had cast me an unkind fate.

I was suddenly turned into a jaguar
and burned with crazed desires,
in my heart was the flame of a menacing fire,
in my muscles the madness of convulsions.

I stole up to a dwelling place
through the empty twilit field
to catch my midnight prey,
as God has fated for me.

But unexpectedly in the dark copse
I saw the tender form of a maiden,
and I remembered her bright earrings,
her doe steps, her glances of a queen.

'The Ghost of Happiness. The White Bride. . .'
I thought, shuddering and confused,
and she declared: 'Don't move from the spot!'
and her look was peaceful and loving.

I was silent, obedient to her call,
I lay, shackled by her signal,
and like a jackal fell prey
to the vicious dogs that hurtled up.

And she walked beyond the woods
with quiet, light steps.
The moon beam circled among her earrings,
the stars talked with the pearls.

For a long time I walked down the corridors
while silence lurked like an enemy all around.
The statues from their niches looked
at the newcomer with hostile stares.

Things were frozen in gloomy sleep,
the grey half-dark was strange,
and my lonely steps sounded
like a malevolent pendulum.

There where the sullen dark was deepest
my burning glance was troubled
by a scarcely visible figure
in the shadow of the crowding columns.

I walked up and then momentary
terror latched onto me like a beast:
my eyes met the head of a hyena
on the elegant shoulders of a girl.

The sharp muzzle was sticky with blood,
the eyes gazed vacantly,
and a hoarse whisper stole forth disgustingly:
'You've come here yourself and now you're mine.'

Terrifying moments coursed
and the half-haze swam.
Innumerable mirrors
repeated the pale terror.

The priest decided. The people, in agreement,
cut my mother's throat:
the lion of the deserts, the beautiful god
waits for me in the heaven of the steppes.

I am not afraid, am I, to hide myself
from the menacing enemy?
I have put on a crimson belt,
amber and pearls.

Here in the desert I call:
'Sun-beast, I have waited so long,
come, prince, and tear
at a human prey.

Let me shudder in your heavy paws
to fall and never rise again,
let me sense the terrible smell,
dark, drunk, like love.

The grasses smell like incense,
I am quiet like a bride,
over my golden bridegroom's
bloodthirsty eyes.'

The gardens of my soul are always ornamental,
in them the winds are so fresh and calmly wafting,
in them are golden sands and black marble
and deep, transparent pools.

The plants in them are unusual as dreams,
the birds are pink as waters at sunrise,
and – who will grasp the hint of an ancient secret? –
in them there is a girl weaving a grand priestess's wreath.

Her eyes are like the sparkle of clean, grey steel,
her exquisite forehead whiter than eastern lilies,
her lips, no one has kissed,
never talked to anyone.

Her cheeks are the roseate pearls of the south,
the treasure of unthinkable fantasies,
and her hands – used to caressing only each other –
are intertwined in the ecstasy of prayer.

By her feet there are two black panthers
whose skins are mottled like metal.
Her flamingo, having flown in from the roses
of a mysterious cave, floats in the azure.

I don't look at the world of running lines,
my dreams only obey the eternal.
Though the sirocco is devilish in the desert,
the gardens of my soul are always ornamental.

PLAGUE

A boat comes into Cairo
flying the long banners of the Prophet.
By looking at the sailors it is not hard
to tell they come from the East.

The captain shouts and bustles,
you can hear his guttural commands.
There are swarthy faces in the rigging
and glimpses of red fezzes.

Children crowd on the quay,
their thin little bodies are funny.
They gathered at dawn
to see where the strangers will moor.

Storks sit on a roof
and stretch their necks,
higher than everybody,
they can see better.

Storks — aerial magi,
they understand many a secret:
why one of the seafarers
has crimson spots on his cheeks.

The storks cry over the houses
but nobody hears the story they tell:
along with the perfumes and silks
into the city has crept — the plague.

Today, I see, you look especially sad,
your arms embracing your knees are especially thin.
Listen: far, far away round Lake Chad
wanders an elegant giraffe.

He is graceful, shapely and languid,
divine gifts – a magical pattern for his skin
that only the moon dares to compete with,
rays breaking and rocking on the waters of broad lakes.

From afar he is like the coloured sails of a ship.
His running flows like a joyful bird's flight.
I know that the earth sees much to marvel at
when he hides in a marble grotto at sunset.

I know the happy tales of mysterious lands
about the black maiden, the young hero's passion,
but you breathed in the heavy mist for too long,
you will not believe in anything except rain.

And how can I tell you of the tropical garden,
of the slender palms, of the smell of undreamed-of herbs.
You are crying? Listen. . . far away round Lake Chad
wanders an elegant giraffe.

On the mysterious Lake Chad,
among the ancient baobab trees,
the carved feluccas of grand Arabs
race along in the sunset.
Ebony-skinned women priests
worship strange gods
by its wooded banks
and in the mountains by the green foothills.

I was the wife of a mighty chief,
the daughter of powerful Chad,
I alone during the winter rain
performed the mysterious rites.
They used to say that for a hundred miles
there was no woman more radiant than me.
I didn't take the bracelets from my arms
and always wore an amber necklace.

The white warrior was so handsome,
red-lipped, with a calm look,
he was a true chief:
and a door opened in my heart,
and when the heart whispers to us
we don't fight, don't wait.
He said scarcely had there been
as enchanting a woman as me
in the whole of France,
and when the sun was rising
he saddled up his Berber
horse for the two of us.

My husband pursued us with his faithful bow,
ran through the wooded thickets,

jumped across the ravines,
swam through the gloomy lakes
and went through mortal agony.
Only the flaming day set eyes on
the corpse of a savage bandit,
a corpse covered in shame.

Whereas I, on a swift and strong camel,
drowning in a caressing mass
of wild animal skins and silken fabrics,
rushed like a bird to the north.
I was snapping my precious fan
in anticipation of the ecstasy to come.
I parted the supple folds
in my many-coloured tent,
and laughing peered out of the little window
and looked at the sun leaping
in the blue eyes of the European.

But now, like a dead fig-tree
whose leaves have all fallen off,
I am a useless, boring lover,
thrown away like an object in Marseilles.
So as to feed myself on pitiful scraps,
so as to live, I dance
in the evenings for drunken sailors
and they laugh – and have their way with me.
My timid mind is overcome with disasters,
my eyes grow dimmer every passing hour. . .
I think of death. But there in unknown fields,
there is my husband – and he waits and does not forgive.

From *Pearls*

When the land cried out at God's injustice
and the barbarians entered the town in a silent horde,
the queen had a couch placed in the crowded square.
The queen waited for the grim barbarians, naked.

Heralds sounded trumpets. Winds whirled the banners
like autumn leaves, rotten, brown leaves.
Gold braid tassels adorned the edges
of rich heaps of Eastern silks and taffeta.

The queen was like a panther of the savage wastes.
Her eyes were chasms of a dark, wild happiness.
Her quivering breasts rose under a pearl bodice,
bracelets trembled on tanned arms and legs.

Her voice sang out like the notes of the silver lyre:
'Make haste, heroes with your bows and slings!
Nowhere will you find a wife more homeless,
whose pitiful groans will be sweeter or more desired!

Make haste, heroes armoured in bronze and steel!
Let the ferocious bolts slam into the poor body
and let your hearts be flooded with fury and sadness,
and be redder than the purple vine clusters.

Long have I waited for you, powerful, rough people,
dreaming and marvelling at the glow of your campfires.
Come, tear my burgeoning breasts, the herald
will sound the trumpet – don't spare the sacred treasures.'

On a bronze tray, slaves brought to the herald
the silver horn adorned with ivory,
but the proud barbarians from the North frowned
and remembered their wandering life in the snow and ice.

They remembered the cold sky and the dunes,
the cheerful chatter of birds in the green thickets,
the royal blue eyes of the women, the strings
that rang with the skalds' songs to woman's majesty.

The broad square seethed and flashed with people,
the Southern sky opened its fiery fan,
but the louring commander reined in his foaming steed
and with a scornful laugh turned his troops to the north.

My troubled soul is tormented
by a strange and terrible question:
can I live on if the son of Atreus died,
dead on a bier of roses?

All that we ever dreamed of —
our longings and terrors —
all was reflected as in limpid water
in those calm eyes.

An inexpressible strength couched in his muscles,
in the groove of his knees — a sweet bliss.
He was beautiful as a cloud,
the king of Mycenae rich in gold.

What am I? The fragment of ancient feuds,
a javelin fallen in the grass,
the son of Atreus, leader of nations is dead,
I, of no worth, live on.

The depths of clear lakes call.
The dawn looks on reproachfully.
This shame is a heavy burden:
to live on when the king is dead.

EAGLE

The eagle flew ever more high and on
to the Almighty's Throne through the stars' thresholds
and his regal flight was beautiful,
his brown feathers were glossy.

Where had he lived before? Perhaps imprisoned
in the shackles of the royal menagerie,
he had screamed, meeting the spring girl
in love with the thoughtful prince.

Or perhaps in a sorcerer's lair,
when he looked through a narrow window,
the heights entranced him
and powerfully transformed his heart into sun.

Isn't it all the same? The azure perfection
was revealed, playing and beckoning;
and he flew for three nights and three days
and died, choking with bliss.

Yes, he died! But he could not fall,
since he'd entered the circles of planetary motion.
The bottomless jaws yawned beneath,
but the forces of gravity were weak.

The vault of the sky was penetrated with rays,
divinely cold rays;
not knowing decay, he flew on
and looked at the stars with his dead eyes.

Worlds went on collapsing into the bottomlessness.
The trump of the archangel sounded on,
ut his grand grave
s not a prey to be played with.

CHRIST

He goes on his pearly way
through the gardens by the shore:
people are busy with unnecessary things,
people are busy with the earthly.

Greetings shepherd! Greetings fisherman!
I'm calling you for eternity,
to see another pasture
and other nets.

Are fish or sheep better
than the human soul?
You, merchants of heaven,
don't count the profits!

A little house in Galilee
is not your reward for work —
but a bright paradise that is pinker
than the pinkest star.

The sun gets close to the zenith,
the winnowing of the end can be heard,
but the Son will rejoice
in the House of the Tender Father.

There's no agonizing over the choice —
what is more captivating than miracles?
The shepherd and the fisherman go
after the heavenly searcher.

The forest in spring is full of song and light,
the fields are black and joyful.
Today for the first time I came across
a crane behind the old hayrick.

I look at the thawing mass,
at the sparkle of pink sunsets,
and my clever cat catches fish
and lures birds into the net.

He knows the tracks of ferret and hare,
the slits that lead through the reeds to the river
and the magpie eggs that are so tasty,
baked in the sand.

When the woods call down the darkness,
the mist drops drops of dew
and I am dozing, the cat purrs,
pushing its wet nose into my hand:

'It's my pleasure to serve you. For you
I will boldly challenge the world,
for you are the Marquis de Karabas,
the descendant of the most ancient races,
the most distinguished of all the Marquises.

The wild animals in the forest, the pines on the mountains,
rich in gold and copper,
the expanse of yellowing wheat fields,
the fish in the depth of lakes,
belong to you as your inheritance.

Why do you sleep in a hole,
always the capricious child,
why don't you live at court
and eat and drink off silver
among the parrots and the lap-dogs?'

My good cat, my clever cat
stifles a sad sigh,
and scratches at fleas angrily
with the claws of his white paw.

In the morning I'm out again under the willow
(I feel so secure by its roots)
and with an absent-minded, lazy hand
throw stones into the smoky pond.

How heavy they are and accurate,
and how they skim over the water!
. . . And in each blade of grass, in each twig
I meet my inheritance.

JOURNEY TO CHINA

To S. Sudeykin

The air is clear and ringing above us,
the ox has carried the grain to the granary,
the lamb has fallen, handed over to the cook,
the wine plays in the bronze ladles.

Why does anguish gnaw at our hearts,
why do we torture our existence?
The best girl cannot give
more than she has.

We have all known angry grief,
we have all abandoned promised paradise,
comrades, we all believe in the sea,
we can sail for distant China.

Only don't think there will be happiness
in the most squawking cockatoo.
The dark child in the tea garden
will fill our soul with burning passion.

We will meet the distance in the pink foam,
the bronze lion frightens us.
What will we dream in the night by the palm
as the juice of trees makes us drunk?

These weeks we spend on the boat
will be a holiday. . .
Are you not experienced in this drunk business,
Master Rabelais, always ruddy-faced?

Heavy as barrels of Tokay wine,
cover your wisdom with a cloak,
you will be the scarecrow of the Chinese girls,
your thighs wound round with green ivy.

Be our captain. We beg you! Beg you!
Instead of an oar we'll entrust you with a sturdy staff.
We'll only anchor in China, although
we may meet death on the way.

I smashed happiness with sacrilegious triumph,
       and there is no anguish, no reproach,
but every night I dream so clearly
       of vast night lakes.
The lilies on the mourning black waves
       are silent as my thoughts,
and the silver-white willows
       arouse forgotten, sad spells.
The moon illumines the bends of the road
       and sees the deserted field,
how I choke in the heavy alarm,
       and wring my hands till they hurt.
I will remember and something must appear,
       like the denouement in a twilight drama:
the sad girl, the white bird
       or a strange, tender fable.
And a new sun will sparkle in the mist
       and the shadows will be dragonflies,
and the proud swans of ancient tales
       will come out on the white steps.
But I can't remember. I am weak, wingless,
       I look at the night lakes
and hear how the waves babble weakly
       the words of the fateful reproach.
I will wake up, my lips confident as before.
       The night is distant and alien,
and the minutes of labour and peace
       are both earthly, beautiful and vulgar.

Today you'll come to me,
      today I will realize
why it is so strange to stay
      alone under the moon.
You will stop, all pale,
      and quietly throw off your cloak.
Isn't that how the full moon
      arises from the dark thickets?
And bewitched by the moon,
      shackled by you,
I will be happy with the silence,
      the dark and the fate.
Thus a beast of the joyless forests,
      sensing the spring,
listens to the rustle of the hours
      and looks at the moon,
and quietly crawls to the gully
      to wake the night's sleep,
and its light pace is in accord
      with the movement of the moon.
Like it I too want to be silent,
      in anguish and in love,
to meet with ancient alarm
      my moon — you.
A moment passes, you are not with me
      and again the day and the dark,
but, burnt by the moon,
      the soul retains your sign.
United bodies
      are parted again,
but like the moon, midnight's
      love is always bright.

Do you remember the palace of the giants,
the silver fish in the pool,
the alleys of tall plane-trees
and the towers of stone rubble?

How a golden horse by the towers
playfully reared up,
and its white saddle-cloth was decorated
with the patterns of slender threads?

Do you remember, by the cavities of clouds
we found a cornice
where the stars, like a bunch of grapes
shot down in a rush?

Now admit, don't turn pale,
we are not now what we were,
perhaps stronger and more bold,
alien only to the dream.

We have beautiful names
like shapely hands,
but the soul is for ever given up
to dead, tormenting boredom.

And we have not yet forgotten,
although it was given us to forget,
that time when we loved,
when we knew how to fly.

KANGAROO

A Girl's Morning

Sleep did not refresh me last night.
I woke early in the morning
and went out, breathing the fresh air,
to look at the tame kangaroo.

It tore off clumps of resinous pine-needles
and chewed them, stupid thing,
and funnily, funnily jumped over to me
and cried out even more funnily.

Its caresses are so clumsy
but I love to caress it,
so that its triumph momentarily
lights its little brown eyes.

Then afterwards, overwhelmed with tenderness
I sat on a bench to daydream;
so is that distant stranger
whom I love not going to appear?

My thoughts lay down so distinctly
like the shadows of leaves in the morning.
I want to caress someone
as the kangaroo caresses me.

PARROT

I am a parrot from the Antilles islands
but I live in the square cell of a magician.
All around – retorts, globes, paper,
the old man coughing, and the ticking of the clock.

In the hours of incantations, in the whirl of voices
and in the sparkle of eyes, flashing like a sword,
let terror and bravery make my wings bristle,
and I fight with the ghosts of owls. . .

Let it be. But when the debaucher in the gilded cloak
enters under this gloomy vault
to tell fortunes from cards or about his love –

I dream of a ship in the quiet of the bay,
I remember the sun. . . and in vain
I yearn to forget that the secret is ugly.

Reader of books — I too wanted to find
my peaceful paradise in obedience to consciousness.
I loved them, those strange ways
where there are no hopes, no memories.

Tirelessly to swim through streams of lines,
to enter hurriedly into the straits of chapters
and watch the foaming of the torrent
and listen to the roar of the incoming tide!

But in the evening. . . Oh, how terrible
is the shadow of night behind the cupboard, the icon-case,
and the pendulum is motionless as the moon
that shines over the glimmering swamp!

Flowers don't live in my home,
I am deceived by their beauty for only a moment,
they last a day or two and then fade,
flowers don't live in my home.

Birds don't live here either,
they only ruffle their feathers mournfully, dumbly,
and in the morning are a little mound of feathers,
even birds don't live here.

Only books in eight rows,
silent, heavy tomes,
guard the age-old languor,
like eight rows of teeth.

The antiquarian bookseller who sold me them,
I remember, was a poor hunchback. . .
The bookseller who sold me them
had his shop beyond the accursed graveyard.

THIS HAPPENED OFTEN

This happened often and will happen again
     in our muted but insistent battle.
As always now you have renounced me,
     tomorrow, I know, you'll return and obey.

But don't be surprised, my feuding friend,
     my enemy, seized by black love,
if the groans of love will be the groans of torture,
     kisses — tinged with blood.

PRAYER

The harsh, threatening sun,
the crazed face
of God in motion in space,
sun, set fire to the present
in the name of the future,
but have mercy on the past!

The palm groves and the aloe thickets,
a silvery, matt stream,
the sky is infinitely blue,
the sky is gold from rays.

What more do you want, heart?
Is happiness a fable or a lie?
Why do you give yourself up submissively
to another faith's temptations?

Do you want poison again?
Do you want to thrash in fiery delirium?
Don't you have the power to live like the grasses
in this intoxicating garden?

One more unnecessary day,
grand and unnecessary!
Come, caressing shadow,
clothe my troubled soul
with your pearl-studded vestments.

You have come. . . You drive away
the malevolent birds – my sadnesses.
O, imperious night,
no one is powerful enough to overcome
the triumphant pace of your sandals!

Silence lands from the stars,
the moon sparkles on your wrist,
and in my dream-sleep I am granted
again the promised land –
happiness that I've cried for for years.

On Arctic and southern seas,
over the hummocks of the green swell,
between basalt and pearly reefs,
the sails of ships rustle.

Dicoverers of new lands, the captains
command the swift-winged ships;
maelstroms and shallows have they known,
hurricanes hold no terrors for them.

The captain's breast is splashed not with dust
of lost charts, but with sea-salt.
He marks his bold course
with a needle on a tattered map,

and going out onto the shuddering bridge,
remembers the port he has left,
slashing off the flecks of foam
from his seaboots with blows of his cane,

or, uncovering a mutiny on board,
whips out a pistol from his belt,
so that gold spills from his cuffs
of pinkish Brabant lace.

Let the sea go berserk and lash,
the crests of the waves rise to the heavens –
not one of them trembles before the storm,
not one reefs his sails.

Are cowards given these hands,
this sharp confident eye
that can suddenly hurl
a frigate against enemy feluccas,

pierce giant whales
with a well-aimed bullet or steel harpoon,
and make out in the starfilled night
the protective beam of lighthouses?

From *Alien Sky*

TO A GIRL

I don't like the languor
of your crossed arms,
your calm modesty
and bashful fear.

Heroine of Turgenev's novels,
you are haughty, tender and pure,
in you is such stormless autumn
from the alley, where the leaves circle.

Don't ever believe in anything,
don't measure before you've calculated,
you will never go anywhere,
unless you can find the route on the map.

That crazy hunter is alien to you,
who having climbed the naked cliff,
in drunken happiness, in unaccountable anguish,
lets go an arrow right at the sun.

Here I am in the quiet evening hour,
I will think of you, only of you.

I take up a book but read 'she'
and again my soul is drunk and troubled.

I throw myself on the creaking bed,
the pillow burns. . . no, I can't sleep, but wait.

I crawl up to the window, look
at the misty meadow and the moon,

over there by the flowerbeds you said 'yes' to me —
this 'yes' is with me forever.

Suddenly consciousness throws me an answer:
that you were never submissive,

that your 'yes', your trembling, your kiss
by the pine tree — were just spring fever and dreams.

Christ said: blessed are the poor;
the fate of the blind, cripples and beggars is to be envied,
I will take them up to the dwelling above the stars,
I will make them knights of heaven
and call them to the most glorious of the glorious. . .
All right! I accept it! But how about those others
whose thoughts we live on and breathe,
whose names call us to action?
How will they atone their greatness,
how will the will to balance all repay them?
Or did Beatrice become a prostitute
and the great Wolfgang Goethe deaf and dumb,
and Byron a vulgar clown. . . Oh God!

The sailors near the port
shouted in chorus, demanding wine,
and over Stambul and over the Bosphorus
the full moon shone.

Tonight they will hurl an unfaithful wife
to the bottom of the bay,
a wife who was too beautiful
and looked like the moon.

She loved her daydreams,
the summer-house in the reed thicket,
old women fortune-tellers and their fortune-telling
and everything the Pasha did not like.

Father was sad, but understands
and whispers to the husband: 'Well, is it time?',
but the younger sister does not lift
her stubborn eyes and muses:

'Many, many other lovers
lie in the deep bays,
intertwined, languid and silent. . .
What happiness to be among them!'

I closed *The Iliad* and sat by the window.
A last word trembled on my lips,
something shone brightly – a streetlamp or the moon,
and the shadow of the watchman slowly moved.

So often I cast a searching look
and so many answering looks met mine –
of Odysseuses in the murk of shipping offices,
of Agamemnons among the tavern gamblers.

So in distant Siberia, where the blizzard howls
mastodons are frozen in the silver ice,
their deep anguish sways the snows there
and the horizons are burnt with red blood.

The book makes me sad, the moon makes me pine.
Perhaps I do not need a hero at all:
a schoolboy and schoolgirl, like Daphnis and Chloe,
walk down the alley and are strangely tender.

SONNET

I must be ill: there's a fog in my heart,
everything bores me — people and stories,
I dream of the queen's diamonds
and a broad-bladed, bloodstained Turkish dagger.

I think (and this is not deception)
my ancestor was a slant-eyed Tartar,
a vicious Hun. I was gripped by the breath
of the plague, transmitted over the centuries.

I'm silent. I pine, and the walls fall back —
here is the ocean all in tatters of white foam,
the granite flooded by the setting sun,

and a city with pale blue domes
and gardens blooming with jasmine,
we fought there. . . Oh yes! I was killed.

From a dragon's lair,
from the town of Kiev,
I took not a wife, but a witch.
I thought: she'll be fun,
and guessed: she'll be capricious,
a happy bird of song.

You call her — she frowns,
you embrace her — she bristles,
and when the moon comes out — she pines,
and she looks and groans,
as though she is burying
someone — and wants to drown herself.

I repeat to her: 'The Lord knows
I haven't got the wizardry
or time to fuss with you.
Take your lassitude off
to the depths of the Dnieper
and to the sinful Bald Mountain.'

She is silent, just hunches up,
and is always unwell.
I pity her, the guilty one,
like a wounded bird,
a blasted birch,
over the bog, cursed by God.

I BELIEVED, I THOUGHT

To Sergey Makovsky

I believed, I thought, and the light flashed on me at last;
the creator, having created me, left me forever to fate;
I am sold! I am no longer God's! The seller went off,
and the buyer looks at me with open mockery.

Yesterday rushes after me like a mountain flying,
and tomorrow waits in front of me like an abyss.
I go on. . . But anytime the mountain will rush into the abyss.
I know, know that my road is a useless one.

And if by my will I bend people to it,
and if inspiration flies to me at nights,
and if I know secrets – the poet, the magician,
the ruler of the universe – then fate will be the more terrible.

Then I dreamed that my heart did not ache,
it is a porcelain bell in yellow China
on a multicoloured pagoda. It hangs and greets with a chime,
teasing the flock of cranes in the enamel sky.

And a quiet girl in a dress of red silks,
where wasps, flowers and dragons are embroidered in gold,
with her knees drawn up, gazes without thoughts and dreams,
attentively listening to the light, light chimes.

'You are completely, completely snow-white,
how strange you are and frighteningly pale!
Why do you tremble as you give
me the glass of golden wine?'

She turned away, sad but sinuous. . .
What I know, I have known for long,
but will drink, drink with a smile
all the wine she has poured me.

Then when the candles are blown out
and nightmares come to my bed,
those nightmares that slowly choke,
I will feel a deadly drunkenness. . .

And I'll come to her and say: 'Darling,
I've had a remarkable dream.
Ah, I dreamed of an endless plain
under a completely gold heaven.

I tell you I won't be cruel any more,
be happy with whomever you want, even him.
I'm going on a long, long journey,
I will not be sad or angry.

I can see the white reflected light of day
from heaven, from this cool heaven. . .
And I am happy, don't cry, my darling,
to know that you poisoned me.'

A shadow flew in. . . The fire was dying down.
He stood alone with his arms on his chest.

His gaze was fixed on the distance
and he bitterly spoke of his sadness:

'I penetrated the depths of unknown countries,
my caravan was on the move for eighty days.

There were chains of menacing mountains, the forest,
and sometimes strange towns in the distance,

and from them in the silence of the night
incoherent howlings would often reach our camp.

We cut wood, we dug ditches —
lions approached us in the evenings,

but there were no cowardly souls among us.
We fired at them, aiming between the eyes.

I dug out an ancient temple from the sand.
My name is given to a river,

and in the land of the lakes five large tribes
obeyed me and honoured my laws.

But now I am weak, as though sleep rules me,
and my soul hurts, it is heavy and hurts.

I have found, have found out what fear is,
buried here inside four walls;

even the flash of gunfire or a wave's splash
are no longer free to break this chain. . .'

The woman in the corner listened to him,
hiding her evil triumph in her eyes.

I will go along the thudding sleepers
        to think and follow
in the yellow sky, in the crimson sky,
        the thread of the running rails.

Trembling, I will wander
        into dull station halls,
until the guard's shout chases
        the ragamuffin away.

Then in a stubborn daydream
        I will remember for the hundredth time
the swift look of a beautiful lady
        sitting in first class.

What does all my love mean
        to her, so proud and distant?
But I'll never see her again
        with her blue eyes, so pale!

I'll tell my secret to a friend,
        I'll tease him
in the warm hour, when the evening
        spreads smoke over the meadows.

With an ugly smile
        he'll answer: 'Come off it!
You've been reading too much rubbish,
        now you're talking it.'

From *Quiver*

It's late. The giants on the tower
ringingly strike three.
The heart is less terrified at night.
Traveller, be quiet and look.

The city is like the voice of a Naiad,
in the transparent-bright past,
the arcades more patterned than lace,
the waters have frozen like glass.

The curtains of black gondolas
must hide witchcraft where
the fires on the lagoon
are a thousand fiery bees.

The lion on the column:
his lion eyes burn bright,
he holds the Gospel of Mark
and is winged as the seraphim.

Where the mosaic sparkles
at the height of the cathedral,
I sense the sighing, cooing
and splash of the doves' chorus.

Perhaps this is just a joke,
the witchery of cliffs and water.
A mirage? The traveller feels awful,
suddenly. . . no one, nothing?

He screamed, but no one heard him,
he tore away, fell
in the shaky pale distances
of the Venetian mirrors.

CONVERSATION

To Georgy Ivanov

When a green ray, the last in the sunset,
flashes and hides itself we can't tell where,
then the soul rises and wanders like a sleepwalker
in the neglected gardens, in the deserted squares.

The whole world is its – and it is not jealous
of the angels or birds in the silence of alleys.
The body drags after and is secretly angry,
complaining gloomily to the earth about its pain.

'How good now to sit in a happy café
where the gas light crackles over the crowd,
and to listen, as I sup my beer,
to a woman singing "La p'tite Tonkinoise".

The cards fly merrily over the tables,
they heal the melancholy, reconcile them to life.
You know, I love to touch gold
with hot hands, when it is mine.'

Think how with this possessed soul
listening to imagined voices,
I can look at the trifling stars; the Almighty
laid out the heavens so plainly.'

At times the earth sighs in sympathy
and smells of resin, dust and grass,
thinks tediously, but nonetheless does not know
how to calm the triumph of the rebellious soul.

'Return to me, child, become again muddy silt
in the depth of marshes, on the cold, slimy bed.
You can choose between the Neva and the Nile
your favourite home for repose.

Let the doors of ears and eyes be closed for ever
and the brain decompose, giving itself up to the enemy,
and after you will become plant or beast. . .
Know that I can't help you in any other way.'

The soul continues, proud of its destiny,
to the non-existent but golden fields,
and the exhausted body hurries after it,
and the earth smells temptingly of decay.

FIVE-FOOT IAMBICS

To M. L. Lozinsky

I remember a night like a black Naiad
on the sea under the sign of the Southern Cross.
I was sailing south: the blades of the propeller
powerfully tore into the mass of the powerful waves,
and the darkness momentarily took away
the vessels we met which delighted our sight.

Oh, how I pitied them, how strange it was for me
to think that they were going back
and had not remained in the undeceiving bay,
that Don Juan had not met Donna Anna,
that Sinbad had not found the mountains of diamonds
and the Eternal Jew was a hundred times more unhappy.

But the months passed. . . I was sailing
back, carrying elephant tusks,
pictures of Abyssinian masters,
panther skins – I liked their spots –
and something that before I never understood:
contempt for the world and tiredness of dreams.

I was young, was hungry and confident,
but the spirit of the earth was silent, arrogant
and the blinding dreams had died
as birds and flowers die.
Now my voice is slow and measured –
I know life was not a success. . . And you,

you, for whom in the Levant I searched
for the undecayed purple of royal mantles,
I lost you, as crazed Nal
once lost Damayanti.
The dice were cast in the air, ringing as steel,
the dice fell – and there was sadness.

You said, pensively and sternly:
'I believed, I loved too much,
I am going away, not believing, not loving,
and before the face of the all-seeing God,
perhaps destroying myself,
I give you up for ever.'

I did not dare to kiss your hair
nor even to squeeze your cold, slender hands.
I was disgusting to myself as a spider,
every sound worried and scared me,
and you went away, in a simple, dark dress,
as at the Crucifixion of old.

That summer was full of storms,
great heat and unusually stifling,
so that it became dark immediately
and the heart would suddenly stop.
The ears of corn shed grain in the fields,
and the sun was crimson even at midday.

In the roar of the crowd,
in the uproar of the passing weapons,
in the incessant call of the military bugle
I suddenly heard the song of my fate
and I ran to where the people were running,
obediently repeating: 'Amen, amen'.

The soldiers sang loudly and the words
were incomprehensible but the heart caught them:
'Quick! Forward! The grave is the grave!
The fresh grass will be our bed;
the green foliage – our canopy,
the archangels' power our ally.'

So sweetly the song flowed and beckoned
that I volunteered and they took me

and gave me a rifle and a horse,
and a field, full of powerful enemies,
menacing buzzing bombs and singing bullets,
and the sky in the lightning, glowing clouds.

My soul since then has been burned
by happiness, full of merriment,
clarity and wisdom, and it talks
with the stars about God,
hears the voice of God in the alarum of battle
and calls its roads Godsent.

Every moment it magnifies
the most honest of honest cherubim,
the most praiseworthy of praiseworthy seraphim,
the heavenly Perfection of earthly hopes,
and senses that its simple words evoke
consideration, grace and benediction.

By the deserted sea there is a monastery
of white stone, golden-domed,
it is lit by an undimming glory.
To go there, to abandon the evil world,
look at the expanse of water and sky. . .
To that golden and white monastery!

JUDITH

From which most wise of Pythians
will the unembellished story
be told about the Jewish woman Judith,
about the Babylonian Holofernes?

Scorched by hot winds
Judaea was in torment for many days —
not daring to argue or obey
before the tents, red as the dawn.

The satrap was powerful with a handsome body,
his voice was like the roar of battle,
but still the girl was not overwhelmed
and her agonized head did not spin.

But at the blessed and accursed hour,
when the bed received them like a whirlpool,
an Assyrian winged bull arose
so strangely unlike the angel of love.

Or perhaps in the smoke of censers soaring
and shrieking to the thunder of the tympani,
from the blackness of the future, Salome
writhed with the head of John the Baptist.

What heights there are over this island,
    what mist!
The Apocalypse was written here
    and here Pan died.

And there are others — with palms, with palaces,
    where the reaper is joyous
and the flocks of sheep tinkle
    their little bells.

Scarcely breathing I took the wondrously bent
    violin into my hands
and listened to its soul running
    into sounds.

Yes! These are only spells that
    defeat me with fate:
at night the starry rain overhead
    and ringing sounds and groans.

I am free, believing in success again,
    the whole world is my home,
I kiss the girl with the hot face
    and the hungry mouth.

But the bridge is lowered to my country from yours
    for just a minute.
Swords, crosses and chalices of huge stars
    will burn it.

BIRD

I don't dare to pray any more,
I have forgotten the words of the litanies.
There is a menacing bird above me,
and its eyes are fires.

Now I hear a restrained screech
as if it were the ringing of rusted cymbals,
as if it were the thunder of a distant sea,
of a sea that beats at the breast of cliffs.

Now I see steel talons
bending over me,
as if, lit by the moon,
the river streams tremble.

I'm afraid. What does it need?
I am not the young Ganymede.
The Greek sky never
streamed its tender light over me.

If this is the dove of the Lord
flown down to say: 'Are you ready!' –
then why is it so unlike
the pigeons in our garden?

I

Like the wind of a happy country
the complaints of those in love carry.
Like the ears of ripened corn
the heads of the unbowed bow.

An Arab sings in the desert:
'They ripped my soul from my body'.
The Greek groans above the blue depths:
'You flew into my soul like a seagull.'

Beauty is their slave!
The Greek woman tends the icon lamps by night,
and the Arab's friend roasts
fragrant beans in the tent.

There is a single call from one land to another,
wider, more wide and more miraculous:
have you divined it, my darling,
in this poor, incoherent song?

Darling, with the summer smile,
with slender, weak hands,
and with your stifling, black hair
like two-thousand-year-old honey.

2

For Adonis with his beauty like the moon,
for slender Hyacinth, for Narcissus,
and for Danaë, the golden cloud,
the Attic heights still mourn.

The breakers of the iambic seas mourn
and the migrating flocks of cranes,
and the palm, about which Odysseus
told troubled Nausicaa a story.

The sad world will not be charmed again
by stifling curls, nor an enticing look,
nor the petals of hot lips, nor blood,
thudding solemnly and wonderfully.

Death is true and life mutters lies. . .
And you, tender one, whose name is song,
whose body music, you too pass on
to merciless disappearance.

But, alas, I don't know the words —
earthquakes, thunder, waterfalls —
that even in death you might live,
like the lads and girls of Greece.

How could we live before in peace
and not wait for joys and disasters,
not dream of the crimson sunset battle,
of the clamouring trumpet of victories?

How could we. . . but it's not too late.
The sun of the spirit has leaned over us.
The sun of the spirit has flooded our skies
serenely yet threateningly.

The spirit flourishes like a May rose,
like fire it cleaves the darkness.
Understanding nothing, the body
blindly obeys it.

In the wild charm of the steppe expanses,
in the quiet mystery of the forest's depths
there is nothing difficult for the will
or harrowing for the soul.

I sense that autumn will soon be here,
the sun's works will end
and people will pluck from the tree of the spirit
golden, ripe fruits.

The patrol passed with swords clanking.
A bad monk stole off to his love.
The unknown rested
on the sharp-roofed houses.

But we are calm, we argue
with the guards about the Lord's anger,
and your broad cloak, Genevieve,
smells of stars and the sea.

Do you remember how the church
rose before us, looming in the dark,
and fiery symbols burnt
over the sombre altars.

Solemn, granite-winged,
it protected our sleepy city,
hammers and saws sang in it —
the masons were working at night.

Their words are few and chance,
but their looks are clear and stubborn.
They know the ancient secrets
of how to build stone churches.

Having kissed the inlaid threshold
and made our genuflection
we asked so submissively
for a blessing on you and me.

The great Master, spirit level in hand,
stood among the crashing and rumble
and whispered: 'Go in peace,
we will conquer Beelzebub.'

While they live on earth
and create the law of holy sowing,
we can boldly be like children
and love each other, Genevieve.

No, I don't envy you and am not
badly hurt that you
        are going away and soon
        will be in the Mediterranean.

You'll see Rome and Sicily,
places beloved of Virgil,
        you'll compose poems of love
        in a fragrant, lemon grove.

More than once I experienced this,
my breast was soaked with sea-salt,
        I composed sonnets to Beatrice
        over the Arno, honouring Dante's custom.

What do nature and antiquity mean to me,
when I am full of burning jealousy?
        You saw in all her attire
        the Muse of Distant Wanderings.

For you the nectar foams in the crystal goblet
in the hands of the treacherous one,
        and you know the lightnings and deliriums
        of fire-breathing conversation.

And I, I am locked away by large
solemn volumes like giants, locked
        in a corner from free life —
        which I can't see or hear.

Today I heard again
how the heavy anchor crawled up,
and I saw the five-decked ferry
sailing out to sea.
That's why the sun breathes
and the earth speaks and sings.

Is there not one rat
in the dirty kitchen, or worm in a hole,
or one toothless and bald man,
obsessed with good,
who doesn't hear the songs of Ulysses
calling him to play?

Oh, to play with Neptune's trident,
with the tresses of the wild Nereids,
in the hour when breakers like strings
break ringingly and the foam shudders
or trembles on the breasts
of the young, most tender of Aphrodites.

Now I come out of my home
to meet a different fate:
the whole world, both alien and familiar,
is ready to be friends with me:
the bends of the shore, the inlets,
and water and sea wind.

The sun of the spirit never sets.
It's not for the earth to fight it.
I will never come back,
I will calm my tired flesh
if the summer is full of grace,
if the Lord loves me.

Midnight has come down — impenetrable darkness,
only the river sparkles in moonlight,
beyond the river an unknown tribe
is lighting bonfires and making noise.

Tomorrow we'll meet and find out
who'll be the masters of these places;
they are helped by the black rock,
we by the gold crucifix on the chest.

Again I look round the hillocks and pits,
here we'll put the baggage, there the mules.
Even trees don't grow
in this gloomy country of Sidamo.

I'm happy to think that if we win —
and we've won many times before —
again the road like a yellow snake
will lead us from hill to hill.

If tomorrow the waves of the Webbe
take my death-sigh into their roar,
dead, I will see the black god
fight with the fiery one in the pale heaven.

1913 *East Africa*

That country that could be paradise
became a lair for fire.
This is the fourth day of our advance,
we have not eaten for four days.

But we don't need earthly food
in this terrible and bright hour,
because the word of the Lord
feeds us better than bread.

The weeks flooded with blood
are blinding and light,
the shrapnel bursts over me,
the sabres soar swifter than birds.

I shout and my wild voice
is bronze striking on bronze,
I, the bearer of a great thought,
cannot, cannot die.

Like thunderous hammers
on the waters of angry seas,
the golden heart of Russia
beats rhythmically in my chest.

It's good to decorate Victory
in pearls like a girl,
pursuing the smoky tracks
of the retreating enemy.

CHINESE GIRL

A pale blue summer-house
in the middle of a river,
like a wicker cage
where butterflies live.

I look at the sunset
from this summer-house,
sometimes I look
at how the twigs rock,

how the twigs rock,
how the boats slide by,
bending past the summer-houses
in the middle of the river.

In my dungeon I have
a bush of porcelain roses,
the tail of a metal bird
sparkles with gold.

Not believing in enticements,
I write on silk
serene tankas
about love and anguish.

My fiancé is more and more in love,
although he's bald and tired,
recently he passed
all his exams in Canton.

Apostle Peter, get your keys,
one worthy of heaven is knocking at the door.

The colloquium of elders of the church
will show that I kept the dogmas.

Let St George tell of how
I fought the enemy in the war.

St Antony can confirm
that I could never pacify my flesh.

But the lips of St Cecilia
will whisper that my soul is pure.

I often dreamed of the gardens of heaven
and the rosy fruit among the branches,

the rays and the voices of angels,
the miracles of nature from outside this world.

Apostle Peter, if I go away
forsaken, what will I do in hell?

My love will melt the ice of hell,
and my tears will flood hell's fire.

The dark seraph will appear
before you to plead my case.

Hurry up now, get your keys,
one worthy of heaven is knocking at the door.

ISLAM

To O. N. Vysotskaya

We were silently drinking Chianti in the night café
when a tall and greying Levantine man came in
and ordered a cherry brandy. He was the most
ferocious enemy of Christians in the whole Levant.

I remarked to him: 'My friend,
stop playing the despicable dandy
at a time when, according to legend,
Damayanti is entering the green dark.'

But he stamped his foot and shouted: 'Women!
You know that the black stone of the Kaaba
was declared fake last week?'

Then he groaned, deep in thought,
and whispered sadly: 'Mice have eaten
three hairs from the Prophet's beard.'

FABLE
For Teffi

There was a castle on the cliff,
at the very edge, where the river Elizabeth
flowed by and bared its rocks like teeth.

The scrawny birds flew to rest
on its battlements and slits,
and cawed dully, forebodingly.

Below, on the slope itself,
lay the lair of the dragon
with six legs and ruddy coat.

The keeper himself was black as tar.
He had long talons
and hid his sinewy tail under a cloak.

He lived modestly, though he was no bear,
and the neighbours knew well
that he was, simply, a devil.

But his neighbours were also
of suspicious coat and skin:
a raven, a werewolf and a hyena.

They gathered and howled
before dawn by the river Elizabeth
and then played dominoes.

Time flew so fast
that a simple nettle seed
managed to turn into a nettle.

This was all in the days before Adam.
Brahma, not God, was living in the heavens,
and turned a blind eye to everything.

If they could only live without sadness!
But one night the hyena and the werewolf
slept together.

They had a child,
half bird and half cat.
The child was happily taken into their company.

They gathered as usual
and having had an excellent wail over the river,
they sat down as always to play.

They played and played and played,
as only they could,
till they were out of breath with stupefaction.

Only the child won everything:
the bottomless beer barrel,
the friends, the lands and the castle.

He shouted out, swelling like a mass:
'Get away all of you from here,
I won't share with any of you!

I'll just put my kind old mother
in that same pit
which was the dragon's lair.'

In the evening by the banks of the Elizabeth
a black carriage passed,
and an old devil sat in the carriage.

Others trailed along behind,
preoccupied and sick,
with hollow coughs and howls.

Some put on a brave face, some whined, others were angry,
and that was when Adam was born.
God save Adam and Eve!

From *Bonfire*

I know that the grandeur of a perfect life
is given to the trees, not to us.
On the dear earth, sister to the stars,
we are on alien ground, they in their fatherland.

Deep autumn comes and in empty fields
the bronze-red sunsets, amber
sunrises teach them colour,
the free, green peoples.

Among the oaks the likes of Moses,
Marys among the palms. . . Their souls, I think,
send one to the other a quiet call
with the water streaming in immeasurable darkness.

Springs burble rapidly in the earth's depth,
sharpening diamond, grinding granite,
springs scream where an elm is chopped down,
sing where a sycamore has been clothed with leaves.

Oh, if only I too could find a land
in which I need not cry and sing,
wordlessly rising to the heights
through the incalculable millennia.

An orange-red sky. . .
The gusting wind rocks
the bloody clusters of the rowan.
I catch up with the horse that's bolted
past the glass of the conservatory,
the barred fence of the old park
and the swan pond.
Alongside me runs
my furry, ginger dog
dearer to me
than my own brother,
and whom I'll always remember
if she were to die.
The beat of hooves multiplies,
the dust rises higher and higher.
It's difficult to pursue
a thoroughbred Arab horse.
You have to sit down,
out of breath
on a broad, flint rock,
and be mutely amazed
at the orange-red sky,
and mutely listen
to the piercing, screaming wind.

CHILDHOOD

As a child I loved the great
meadows, fragrant with honey,
the glades, the dry grasses
and the bull's horns among the grass.

Each dusty bush by the wayside
shouted at me: 'I'm joking with you,
go round me carefully
and you'll see who I am!'

Only the wild autumn wind
blustered, then stopped its game.
My heart beat even more blissfully
and I believed that I'd die –

not alone, but with my friends,
the coltsfoot, the burdock,
and beyond the distant skies
I could suddenly divine everything.

This is why I love the exploits
of war's menacing games:
that human blood is no more sacred
than the emerald juice of the grass.

The islands have already clothed themselves
with transparent spring greenery,
but no, the Neva is changing,
it's so easy for it again to become gloomy.

Go onto the bridge, look down:
there the ice floes leap on ice floes,
green like copper poison,
with the terrifying rustle of a snake.

These are what weigh on a geographer's
mind, in the hour of difficult dreams —
the troublesome outlines
of unknown continents.

So those secret cellars
smell with the damp of mushrooms,
hesitantly and weakly,
where a corpse is buried and toads wander round.

The river is sick, the river is fevered.
Only the white bears are content
in the zoological garden,
confident in their victory.

They know that their tough incarceration
is only a deception.
The icy Arctic
is coming to their rescue.

Yes, I know, I am not worthy of you.
I come from a foreign land,
and I like the savage melody
of the *zourna* not the guitar.

I read my poems not
to dark dresses and jackets
in halls and salons, but
to dragons, waterfalls, clouds.

I love – as an Arab in the desert
falls to the water and drinks,
and not like a knight in a picture,
who watches the stars and waits.

I will not die in bed
in a notary's and a doctor's presence,
but in some wild ravine
drowned in thick ivy,

so that I won't enter a wide open,
Protestant, ordered heaven,
but go where the robber, the publican
and the whore cry: 'Arise!'

THE PEASANT

There are strange peasants
in the forests and the vast marshes,
living in mossy and dark huts
near the tin-panning river.

One of them sets out into the wasteland
where the feather-grass has run wild.
He hears the screech-owl's cries
and senses ancient lore.

The Tartar passed through here
and his look is here to stay.
There is a sense of damp and snakes
beside the shallow rivers.

Here he is with his traveller's bundle,
filling the forest road
with his long-drawn-out song, soft
but villainous, villainous.

This road is light and dark,
thieves whistle in the open field,
and there are arguments and bloody fights
in nightmarish taverns.

He enters the proud capital,
oh Lord preserve us,
and puts a spell on the Tsaritsa
of boundless Russia

with a look and a childish smile
and his so mischievous words,
and on his dashing chest
a gold cross shone.

How did the cross on Kazan
Cathedral not bend, oh Lord,
how did the cross
on St Isaac's not leave its place?

Gunshots, screams, sirens
over the shocked capital.
The city gnashed its teeth
like a lioness protecting her cubs.

'Orthodox men and women, you can burn
my corpse on the dark bridge,
and cast the ashes to the wind. . .
Who will defend the orphan?

In this wild, poverty-stricken country
there are many peasants like me,
and your roads rumble
with their gleeful footsteps.'

He stands in front of the red-hot furnace,
a short, old man.
His blinking reddish eyelids
give his calm look a submissive air.

All his mates have gone to sleep,
he alone is still awake.
He is still busy casting the bullet
that will part me from the earth.

Finished, and his eyes brighten up.
He goes back home. The moon shines.
His sleepy, warm wife
waits for him in their big bed.

The bullet cast by him will whistle
over the hoary, foaming Dvina.
The bullet cast by him will search out
my chest, it has already come for me.

I will fall in mortal anguish.
I will see the past face to face.
My blood will gush out onto the dry,
dusty, crushed grass.

And the Lord will pay me in full measure
for my brief bitter life.
This is what the short old man
in the light grey blouse has done.

Oh yes, we are a race
of ancient conquerors,
bearing over the North Sea
a broad, painted sail,
and jumping from the long-boats
onto the flat Normandy shore
to bring fire and death
into the lands of the old princedoms.

It's more than one century
we've been wandering the world,
we wander and trumpet our trumpets,
we wander and beat our drums:
'Do you need strong arms,
do you need hard hearts,
and do you need red blood
for Republic or King?

Heh, boy, bring us
drink quickly,
Malaga or port,
but above all – whisky!'
What's that there:
a submarine,
a floating mine?
This is what sailors are for!

Oh yes, we are from a race
of ancient conquerors,
who are fated constantly to be on the move,
to fall from high towers,
to drown in the hoary oceans,
and with our violent blood

to feed those insatiable drunkards:
iron, steel and lead.

But still the poets compose
songs in different languages
both western and eastern.
But still the monks pray
in Madrid and Mount Athos,
like candles burning before God,
but still the women dream —
of us and only us.

Whoever lies in the grave
hears a wonderful ringing
and senses the smell
of the whitest lilies.

Whoever lies in the grave
sees an eternal light,
the transfused snow
of the Seraphim wings.

Yes, you are dying,
your hands are cold,
and you yourself don't know
the unearthly spring.

But you're going to heaven
according to my prayer,
this is so, I know,
I promise you.

You are not always alien and proud
and you don't always not want me,

softly-softly, tenderly as in a dream
you sometimes come to me.

There is a thick lock on your brow,
I am forbidden to kiss it.

Your big eyes are burnt
by the light of the magical moon.

My tender friend, my merciless enemy,
every step of yours is blessed

as though you are walking on my heart,
scattering stars and flowers.

I don't know where you got them from,
only why are you so bright;

and for him who could be with you
is there nothing left to love on this earth?

About you, you, you,
nothing, nothing about me!
You are the winged appeal to the heights
in our dark, human fate.

Your noble heart
is like a crest of times past.
It sanctifies the existence of all earthly,
all wingless generations.

If the stars are clear and proud
and turn away from our earth,
it still has two better stars:
and they are your bold eyes.

When the golden seraph
trumpets out that the time has come,
then we will raise before him
your white handkerchief as a defence.

The trumpet will sound. The noise will die down.
The seraph will disappear in the heights.
About you, you, you,
nothing, nothing about me!

DREAM

I groaned from a bad dream
and woke up in heavy sadness,
I dreamed you loved another
and that he had hurt you.

I ran from my bed
like a murderer from his scaffold
and I saw how the streetlamps
glittered dully with the eyes of beasts.

Oh, no one ever wandered
so homelessly that night
down the dark streets,
as down beds of dried-up rivers.

Here I am standing before your door:
I have no other path,
although I know that I will never
dare go through this door.

He hurt you, I know,
although this was just a dream,
but nonetheless I am dying
in front of your closed window.

How strange – it is exactly ten years
since I saw Ezbekie,
the big park in Cairo, solemnly
illuminated that evening by the full moon.

A woman then was the cause of my misery
and neither the fresh, salt wind from the sea,
nor the crashing commotion of exotic bazaars:
nothing could comfort me.
I prayed to God about death,
and was ready myself to hasten its coming.

But this garden, it was exactly like
the sacred groves of the young world:
there the slender palms put out branches,
like girls to whom God comes down;
the grand plane-trees crowded
on the hills, like druid prophets,

and the waterfall was white in the dark,
just like a unicorn prancing:
the moths flew around
among the flowers which were raised high,
or among the stars – the stars hung that low
like ripe barberries.

And I remember I exclaimed: 'Life is higher
than grief, deeper than death. Accept
this wilful covenant of mine: whatever would happen,
whatever sadnesses, humiliations
should fall to my lot, I will not
think about an easy death before
once again I enter on such a moonlit night
under the palms and plane-trees of Ezbekie.'

How strange – exactly ten years have passed
and I cannot stop myself thinking of the palms
and plane-trees, and of the waterfall,
of the spray – white as a unicorn,
and suddenly I look round, hearing
in the wind's howling the noise of distant speech,
and in the horrific silence of the night
the mysterious word, Ezbekie.

Yes, only ten years, but I, the frowning wanderer,
must travel there again, must see
the sea and clouds and strangers' faces –
everything that no longer enthralls me,
and must enter that park, repeat my covenant
or say that I have fulfilled it
and that now I am free.

From *The Porcelain Pavilion*

Chinese Poems

A porcelain pavilion stands
in the artificial lake;
a bridge of jasper leads to it,
convex, like a tiger's back.

In the pavilion a few friends
dressed in bright clothes
drink mulled wine from cups
decorated with dragons.

They talk together happily,
write down their verses
tilting their yellow hats,
rolling up their long sleeves.

The curved bridge like a jasper moon
is reflected brightly in the clear lake,
and behind their cups
a few friends upside down.

The moon has already left the cliffs,
the sea is full of transparent gold,
a few friends on a sharp-prowed boat
take their time to drink the mulled wine.

Watching the light clouds pass through
the moon's column reflected on the sea
some of them muse that this is
a procession of the grand Khan's women;

others believe that they are the shades
of god-fearing people going off to the groves of heaven;
and others argue with them saying
it is a caravan of swans.

Joyful heart, winged heart.
In my light, small boat
I skim over the freedom of the ripples
all day from dawn to sunset
and love the reflection of the mountains
on the surface of clear lakes.

Formerly a thousand troubles engulfed me,
my heart beat like a beast at bay,
and longed for unknown distances
and longed for. . . But now
I love the reflection of the mountains
on the surface of clear lakes.

The small lake is calm
like a cup full of water.

Bamboos just like huts,
trees like a sea of roofs.

Sharp rocks, like pagodas,
rear up among the flowers.

I am happy to think that
eternal nature learns from us.

Lawful Wife

In the deep cup there is still wine
and swallows' nests are on the dish.
The mandarin has respected his lawful wife
from the beginning of the world.

Concubine

In the deep cup there is still wine
and a big fat goose on the dish.
If the mandarin has no children,
the mandarin will take a concubine.

Maidservant

In the deep cup there is still wine
and choice jams are on the dish.
You may both be the mandarin's,
but he wants a new woman every night.

Mandarin

There is no more wine in the deep cup,
only a red pepper on the dish.
Stop your stupid prattling,
don't laugh at an unhappy old man.

My boat is of red wood,
my flute of jasper.

Water brings out a stain from silk,
wine — sadness from the heart.

And if you master the light craft,
wine and sweet woman,

what more do you need? In all things
you are like the genii of the heavens.

From *Tent*

Flocks of days and nights
have cast spells over me,
but I have never known brighter ones
than on the Suez canal,

where the ships sail
not over the sea but over pools
in the middle of the land
like a caravan of camels.

How many birds, how many birds
there are here on the rocky slopes,
pale blue fables,
large-cropped waders.

Golden-green, a swarm
of lizards can be seen,
as though the spray of the sea
had cooled on the slopes.

We throw fruit
as we pass the Arab children
who sit by the water,
pretending to be pirates.

The black children shout
so fervently and ringingly,
and the marabou hisses
curses after us.

When night settles
like a vulture on the sands,
the little fires flicker
before and behind us.

Those are redder than coral,
these are green, blue. . .
a watery carnival
in the African desert.

From distant hills, the smoke
of Bedouin fires
comes down to us,
chased by the light wind.

The cackles of hyenas,
the howling of jackals are heard
from the collapsed walls
and the bends of the canal.

In answer the steamer,
saddening the night stars,
sends flourishes from a piano
to sleeping Africa.

I pitched my tent on the stony slope
of the Abyssinian mountains that run to the west,
and carefreely watched the sunsets flaring
over the green roof of the distant forests.

Some birds flew from there
with emerald feathers in their long tails.
By night the joyous zebras ran out:
I heard them panting and the blows of their hooves.

Once the sunset was especially red
and a special smell flew from the forests.
A European came up to my tent.
He was gaunt, unshaven and asked for food.

He ate clumsily and hungrily into the night,
put sardines on a piece of dry meat.
He swallowed Maggi cubes like pills
and refused water for his absinthe.

I asked why he was so deadly pale
and why his withered hands shook
like leaves. 'The fever of the great forest'
he answered and looked over his shoulder in horror.

I asked about the big open wound
that showed black through the rags on his sunken chest,
how did it happen? 'A gorilla of the great forest'
he said and did not dare look back.

There was a pigmy with him, waist-high, naked and black,
it seemed to me that he could not speak.
Like a dog, he sat behind his master,
leaning his bulldog face on his knees.

But when my servant jostled him for fun
he bared his terrible teeth
and then was upset for the whole day and snorted
and beat the earth with his painted spear.

I offered a bed to the exhausted guest,
lay on panther skins, but couldn't sleep,
hungrily listening to the long wild story,
the feverish deliriums of the stranger from the forest.

He growled: 'How dark it is, this eternal forest . . .
We'll never see the sun again. . .
Pierre, have you got the diary? Next to you, under your shirt?
Better to lose our lives than that diary!

Why have the black men abandoned us?
My God, they've taken our compasses. . .
What can we do? We can see neither beast nor bird
but there's a whistling and rustling above and below!

Pierre, have you spotted the bonfires? There must be. . .
Are we saved at last?
They're pigmies. . . look how many have gathered. . .
Fire, Pierre. There's a human foot in the fire!

Hand to hand! Remember the arrows are poisoned!
Hit the one on the stump, he's shouting, he's their leader. . .
Oh my God, my rifle's smashed. . .
I'm done for. . . they've overwhelmed me.

No, I'm alive, only tied up. . . evil bastards!
Let me go, I can't watch it!
They're roasting Pierre. . . We played together in Marseilles,
we played as children on the cliff by the sea.

What do you want, dog? You're kneeling down.
I spit on you, horrible beast.
But you're licking my hand. Are you tearing the rope?
Yes, I understand, you think I'm a god. . .

Quick, let's run! Don't take human meat,
the almighty gods don't eat it. . .
The forest . . . oh the eternal forest . . . I'm hungry, Akka,
catch me if you can a big snake!'

He groaned and wheezed, he clutched at his heart
and in the morning he seemed to have fallen asleep;
but when I tried to wake him, I saw
flies crawling over his eyes.

I buried him by the foot of a palm tree.
I placed a cross on a pile of heavy stones
and wrote these simple words on a board:
'A Christian is buried here, pray for him.'

The pigmy, cleaning his spear, looked on impassively,
but when I had completed the sad rites
he jumped up and without a shout raced down the slope
like a deer running off to its native forests.

A year later I read in the French newspapers,
I read this and in sadness hung my head:
'Up till now no one has returned
from the grand expedition to the Upper Congo.'

From *Blue Star*

From a whole bouquet of lilac
I got just one lilac bloom,
and all night I thought about Helen,
and then pined the whole day through.

It seemed to me that the dear earth
was disappearing in white foam,
damp lilacs were blossoming
beyond the stern of a big ship.

And beyond the fiery skies
she was thinking about me:
the girl with gazelle eyes
of my most favourite dream.

My heart bounced, like a child's ball,
I trusted the ship like a brother,
because it couldn't be any other way,
because I love her.

We flew through bright alleys,
we flew near the water,
the golden leaves fell
into sleepy, blue ponds.

She entrusted to me
her whims, dreams and thoughts,
everything that a girl can dream up
about a still unknown love.

She said: 'Yes, love is free,
and a person is free in love,
but the only heart that is noble
is the one that knows how to love forever.'

I looked in her big eyes
and I saw a sweet face
in a frame where the golden trees
flowed with the waters in one ring.

And I thought: 'No, love is not this!
In fate love is like a forest fire,
because even without an answer
I am fated to you from now on.'

Probably in a former life
I murdered my father and mother,
since in this one – O everpresent God –
I am so cruelly condemned to suffer.

If I were to call my dog,
if I were to look at my horse,
the beasts would run away from me,
not obeying my sign.

If I were to walk up to the foaming sea
that I've known for so long and is so close to me,
the sea would turn black with grief
and swiftly retreat before me.

My every day is calm as a dead man,
all my actions are alien to me, there is only
the torpor of a completely unworthy,
completely Platonic love.

Let the languor of death come to me,
it won't get in the way of my waiting,
so that in my future reincarnation
I will become a warrior again.

Just black velvet, on which
a shining diamond is forgotten:
that's all I can compare with the look
of her eyes that almost sing.

Her porcelain body
languishes with a vague whiteness
like petals of white lilac
under the dying moon.

Her hands may be tender and waxen,
but the blood in them is as hot
as the inextinguishable candle
before the icon of the Virgin Mary.

In sum, she is light as a bird
in the clear days of autumn,
ready now to say farewell
to the sad northern country.

The golden night was flying by
but paused for a while on its way,
it wanted to help me like a friend
and thought about finding your letters:

those which you didn't write me. . .
Then it sat down on my bed
and said: 'You know it's good
to dream a bit in the stillness!

That other one is quite wicked,
she is too lazy even to meet you.
Love me: I am bright,
so bright that I outshine the day.

Many black roses bloom
in my secret wells,
the sparks of blue flame dance
like the wings of fiery dragonflies.

It's the same flame that is in your eyes
at the moment when you think of her. . .
It's for you that I hold back
my black, stubborn horses.'

Night, I pray, don't torture me.
Even without that my fate is heavy.
Don't you realize that if I could
I would have left her long ago?

I mourn now with a mortal sorrow
but what answer can I give
before I tell her 'I love you'
and she answers me 'No'.

Monotonous, my days flash past
all with the same pain,
as though roses are falling
and nightingales dying.

But she is sad as well, the one
who commanded me to love —
and under her satin skin
poisoned blood runs.

If I live in this world
it is only because of one dream:
like blind children, we both
will go up into the mountain heights,

there, where only the goats roam
in a world of whitest clouds,
to search for faded roses
and listen to dead nightingales.

The soul dozed like a blind person,
this is how dusty mirrors sleep,
but you entered the dark heart
like the sunny cloud of paradise.

I didn't know that the heart held
so many blinding constellations,
so as to beg God for happiness
for your eyes that speak.

I didn't know that the heart held
so many ringing harmonies,
so as to beg God for happiness
for your half-childish lips.

I am happy that the heart is rich,
your body, I know, is fire,
your soul is wondrously winged –
and you are my song.

Your tormenting, miraculous
inevitable beauty
tore me out of crowded life,
so poor and simple.

I died. . . and saw a flame
that had never been seen before:
before my blinded eyes
a blue star shone.

Transforming spirit and body,
a melody rose and fell again.
Your blood talked and rang out
like a singing lute.

There was a smell, more fiery and sweet
than anything I'll find in life,
even more so than the lily that stands
in the lofty garden of the angels.

Suddenly the earth came back
from the radiant depth.
You trembled before me
like a wounded bird out of the blue.

You kept saying: 'I'm suffering',
but what can I do, when
I know so sweetly, so finally:
that you are just a blue star.

My heart had fought for so long,
my tired eyelids had stuck together,
I thought I had lost my voice,
my resonant voice forever.

But you returned it to me,
it belongs to me once more,
and again there is the flash of white lilies
and blue worlds in the memory.

I know all the roads
on this far-flung earth. . .
But your darling legs are covered
in blood, and it hurts you to run.

Some malevolent pendulum
rules over our fate,
swings like a sword between
joy and anguish.

That moment when I am happy
with my song brings you suffering.
When you are happy – I regret
the day I was born.

I said: 'Do you want me, want me?
Can I be loved by you?
You prophesy a strange happiness
with your throaty voice.

I pay much for happiness,
my home is of stars and songs,
and sweet alarm will grow
at the sound of your name.'

They will say: 'What is he? Only a violin,
sobbing submissively, that's what he is.
Her smile alone gives birth
to this wonderful melody.'

They will say: 'It is the moon and the sea,
light doubly reflected,'
and after: 'O what a disaster
that there is no other woman the same.'

With not one word in answer
she passed by pensively,
she did me no ill,
and life is bright as before.

The seraphim descend to me,
I sing to the midnight and the day,
but instead of the woman I love
I preserve a dried flower.

A tenderly unprecedented joy
lightly touched my shoulder
and now I need nothing,
I want neither you, nor happiness.

One thing I would accept without question —
quiet, quiet golden peace
and twelve thousand feet of sea
above my pierced head.

Just think how sweetly would that peace
caress and that roar eternal lull,
if only I had never lived,
had never sung nor loved.

HAIKU

So the girl with gazelle eyes
is marrying an American.
Why did Columbus discover America?

The Pillar of Fire

Only snakes shed their skins
so that their souls may age and grow.
We, alas, are not like snakes,
we change our souls, not our bodies.

Memory, with the hand of a giantess
you lead life like a horse by the bridle,
you will tell me about those souls
who lived in this body before me.

The very first was thin and ugly,
loved only the twilight of the woods,
a fallen leaf, a witch's child,
who could stop the rain with a single word.

A tree and a ginger dog —
these were the friends he took.
Memory, Memory, you will find no sign,
you will not convince the world that this was me.

And the second. . . He loved the wind from the south,
in every sound he heard the strings of the lyre,
he said that life was his true friend,
that the rug under his feet was the world.

I don't like him at all, he's the one
who wanted to become a god or king.
He hung a sign saying 'poet'
over the doors of my silent house.

I love the chosen one of freedom,
the seafarer and sharp-shooter,
how sonorously the waters sang to him,
how the clouds envied him.

His tent was tall,
the mules were frisky and strong,
like wine he imbibed the sweet air
of the land unknown to white men.

Memory, you are weaker year by year.
Was it he or someone else
who exchanged the joys of freedom
for the sacred long-awaited war?

He knew the tortures of hunger and thirst,
troubled sleep, the endless road.
The St George Cross twice touched
his breast that was untouched by any bullet.

I am the pensive, stubborn architect
of this temple rising from the gloom.
I was zealous for the glory of the Father
on earth as well as in Heaven.

My heart will burn with flames
till the day when the bright walls
of the New Jerusalem rise up
on the fields of my native land.

Then a strange wind will blow —
a terrible light will flow from the sky,
and the Milky Way will burst into blossom
in a garden of blinding planets.

An unknown traveller will appear before me,
his face hidden: but I will understand everything
when I see the lion rushing in pursuit
and the eagle flying towards him.

I will cry out that my soul should not die –
but will anyone help?
Only snakes shed their skins,
we change our souls, not our bodies.

In that forest whitish trunks
loomed unexpectedly out of the gloom,

root after root came out of the ground
like the arms of grave-dwellers.

Under the cover of bright fiery foliage
lived giants, dwarfs and lions

and the fishermen saw tracks in the sand
of a six-fingered human hand.

No path ever brought here a knight
of France or the Round Table,

no robber had nested in these bushes,
no monk had dug out caves here.

Only once on a stormy night
a cat-headed woman went out,

wearing a crown of cast silver,
and groaned and sighed till morning

and died a quiet death at dawn
before the priest had given her the last rites.

This happened, happened in those times
which have left no trace.

It happened, happened in a land
which you couldn't dream of even in your dreams.

I dreamed this up, looking at your plaits
that coil like a fire-breathing snake,

looking at your greenish eyes,
a sick Persian turquoise.

Perhaps that forest is your soul,
perhaps that forest is my love,

or perhaps when we die
the two of us will go into that forest.

On that day of old, when God inclined
his face over the new world,
then the Word could stop the sun,
the Word could destroy towns.

And the eagle did not flap its wings,
the stars huddled up to the moon in horror,
when the Word – like a roseate flame –
sailed in heaven's height.

And there were numbers for lowly life
like domestic and yoked cattle,
because an intelligent number
conveys all shades of meaning.

A grey-haired patriarch who had brought
both good and evil under his sway
daring not to turn to sound,
traced a number in the sand with his cane.

But we forgot that in the trials and tribulations
of this world only the Word is radiant,
and in the Gospel according to St John
it is said that the Word is God.

It is we who have imposed on it
the meagre limits of nature,
and like bees in a deserted hive
dead words smell bad.

1

The night silence floats over the town
and every rustle becomes more dull,
and you, soul, still you are silent.
Have mercy, Lord, on marble souls.

As though distant harps began to play,
my soul answered me:
'Why did I ever open my eyes to existence
in this contemptible human body?

Out of my mind, I abandoned my home,
yearning for another magnificence,
and the globe of the earth became the ball
to which a convict was chained.

Oh, I came to hate love –
it's an illness which has all of you under its spell,
which clouds again and again
a world alien to me, but harmonious, beautiful.

If there is something that still links me
with the past glimmering in the planetary choir,
then it is grief, my trusted shield,
cold, contemptuous grief.'

2

The golden sunset became like bronze,
the clouds were covered in green mildew,
and then I said to the body: 'Answer
to all that the soul proclaimed.'

My body answered me,
my simple but hot-blooded body:
'I don't know what existence means
although I know what is called love.

I love to splash in the salt waves,
to listen to the hawks' cries.
I love to gallop on an unbroken horse
over the caraway-scented meadow.

And I love a woman, when I kiss
her lowered eyes. I am drunk
as though a thunderstorm is approaching
or as if I drink spring water.

But for everything I've taken or want,
for all the sadnesses, joys and ravings,
I shall pay, as a man must,
with my final, irrevocable death.'

3

When the word of God sparkled
from the heights like the Great Bear
with the question: 'Who are you, questioner?' —
the soul and body appeared before me.

I gave them a slow look,
and graciously answered boldly:
'Tell me, is the dog rational
when he howls at the bright moon?

Is it your rôle to interrogate me,
me for whom a single moment
is the whole span from the first day on earth
to the fiery end of the world?

Me, who like the tree of Yggdrasil
grew with the crown of seven times seven universes,
and for whose eyes the fields of the earth
and the Elysian fields are like dust?

I am one who sleeps and the deep covers
his inexpressible name,
and you, you are only the weak reflection of a dream,
running in the depth of its consciousness!'

A shout came loudly
in a blue-black dream —
in my yard there is a red
and winged fire.

The wind is sweet and wild,
it flew in from the moon,
lashes boldly and painfully
at the cheeks of silence.

The young dawn, stepping
onto the steep slopes
feeds the hungry storm clouds
with amber oats.

I was born at this hour,
at this hour I'll die
and so I never dreamed
of the way that leads to good.

My lips only find happiness
in kissing just one,
her, with whom there is no need
to fly into the heights.

We're not at all in this world, but somewhere
in the backyards of the world among the shades.
Summer sleepily leafs through
the blue pages of clear days.

The pendulum, pushy and vulgar,
the unacknowledged bridegroom of time,
cuts off the beautiful heads
of the plotting seconds.

Each road is so dusty here,
each bush so wants to be withered,
that the white seraph will not lead
the unicorn to us by the bridle.

My darling, only in your precious sadness
is there a fiery ecstasy
which in this accursed backwater
is like the wind from far-off lands.

There where all is sparkling, movement,
singing — that's where you and I live.
But here the stagnant watering-hole
has only imprisoned our reflections.

Because of your words, like nightingales,
because of your words, like pearls,
my words are wild beasts
with rough fur, tusks and horns.

I have gone mad, my beauty.

Because of your cheeks, Shiraz roses,
I have lost the colour in my cheeks,
for your golden hair
I have scattered my gold.

I have become completely naked, my beauty.

So as to see but once
whether your look is of turquoise or beryl,
for seven nights I didn't close my eyes,
did not go away from your gates.

My eyes have become bloodshot, my beauty.

Because you are always at home
I don't come out of the tavern.
Because you are proud of your honour
my hand is drawn to the knife.

I have become a street hooligan, my beauty.

If there is a sun and God is eternal,
then you will step over my threshold.

When I finally finish
the game of *cache-cache* with grim death,
then the Creator will make of me
a Persian miniature.

The sky will be like a turquoise,
the prince will scarcely lift
his almond eyes
to the flight of the maiden's swing.

There'll be a shah with a bloody spear
rushing down the uncertain path
on the cinnabar heights
after the chamois that's in flight.

There'll be tuberoses never seen before,
neither in dreams nor reality,
and in the sweet evening in the grass
the vines will bend to the ground.

On the other side,
pure as the clouds of Tibet,
it will be my joy to carry
the mark of a great artist.

A fragrant old man,
a merchant or a courtier
will fall for me at one glance
with a sharp and steady love.

I will be the guiding star
of his monotonous days,
I will replace in turn
wine, lovers and friends.

And that's when I will quench
without rapture, without suffering,
my old dream's thirst:
to arouse adoration everywhere.

There is beauty in the wine that loves us,
and the good bread which is in the oven,
and the woman whose lot it is
to wear us down then delight us.

But what can we do with the pink sunset
over the cooling heavens
where there is silence and an unearthly peace,
what can we do with immortal poems?

They can't be eaten, drunk, or kissed.
The moment speeds inexorably away
and though we wring our hands,
again we are fated to lose.

Just as a boy forgets his games
and watches the girls bathing,
and knowing nothing about love
is still tortured by mysterious desire;

just as once a slippery creature
sliding through rank undergrowth,
feeling on its back unformed wings
roared when it realized its impotence;

so age after age – how soon, O Lord? –
under nature and art's scalpel
our spirit screams, our flesh is exhausted,
giving birth to the organ of the sixth sense.

My love for you is now a baby elephant
who was born in Berlin or Paris
and treads with padded feet
the rooms of the menagerie owner.

Do not offer him French rolls,
do not offer him cabbage stumps,
he can eat just a quarter of a mandarin,
a lump of sugar or a sweet.

Don't cry, my darling, because in a cramped
cage he will be the crowd's laughing-stock,
and when shop assistants blow their cigar smoke
into his face, the working girls will giggle.

Don't think, my dear one, that the day will come
when he'll go crazy and break his chain,
and run down the streets and squash
screaming people like a bus.

No, may you see him in a dawn dream,
in brocade and bronze, in ostrich feathers,
like that splendid one who once
carried Hannibal towards trembling Rome.

I was walking along an unfamiliar street
when I suddenly heard the cawing of crows,
the ringing of a lute and distant thunder —
a tram was flying past.

How I jumped on its step
was a mystery to me.
It left a fiery trail in the air
even in broad daylight.

It rushed like a dark, winged storm.
It lost its way in the abyss of time. . .
Driver! Stop!
Stop the tram immediately!

Too late. We have already rounded a wall,
hurtled through a palm grove,
thundered over three bridges —
across the Neva, the Nile and the Seine.

And, in a flash past the window,
an old beggar — of course the very one
who died a year ago in Beirut —
threw us a searching glance.

Where am I? So languidly, so anxiously
my heart beats in answer:
do you see the station where you can buy
a ticket for the India of the Spirit?

A signboard. . . the letters flooded with blood
spell out: '*Greengrocer*'. I know that
instead of cabbages and swedes
they sell dead heads here.

In a red shirt, with a face like an udder,
the executioner cut off my head as well.
It lay together with the others
at the very bottom of the slippery box.

A wooden fence by the side-street,
a three-windowed house and a grey lawn.
Driver! Stop!
Stop the tram immediately!

Mashenka, you lived and sang here,
wove a rug for me, your betrothed.
Where now are your body and voice,
can it be that you are dead?

How you moaned in your chamber,
while I, with hair powdered,
went to present myself to the Empress,
never to see you again.

Now I understand: our freedom
is only a light penetrating from another world.
People and shadows stand by the entrance
to the zoological garden of the planets.

And a familiar sweet wind rises suddenly,
beyond the bridge a rider's hand
in a mailed glove — and two hooves
of his horse fly after me.

St Isaac's is carved on high,
the true stronghold of Orthodoxy;
there I will order prayers to be said
for Mashenka's health, and a requiem for me.

But still my heart is forever gloomy,
it's difficult to breathe, living is painful. . .
Mashenka, I never thought that
one could feel such love and such sadness.

'Elga, Elga!' – resounded over the fields
where muscled young men
with savage blue eyes
smashed each other's spines.

'Olga, Olga!' the Drevlyane shouted,
with hair blonde as honey,
scratching their way in the red-hot torture tubs
with bloodied fingernails.

Beyond the foreign, distant seas
the Varangian steel in Byzantine bronze
was never too tired to ring out
the same resonating name.

I have forgotten all I remembered before,
the names of Christians,
and only your name, Olga, is sweeter
than any vintage wine to my throat.

The centuries sing out in the blood,
more inevitably, year after year.
I am drunk with the earlier heaviness
of Scandinavian skeletons.

A warrior relic from ancient struggles,
hiding my enmity to this life,
I wait for the crazed vaults of Valhalla,
the glorious battles and feasts.

I see a skull full of heady beer,
the pink backbones of bulls;
and, a Valkyrie, you circle
above me – Olga, Olga.

The fat man rocked as if on drugs.
His teeth sparkled under his menacing moustache,
knots of gold braid wound
on his bright-red Hussar's uniform.

A string twangs. . . and a throaty scream. . .
and straight away my blood moaned so sweetly,
I believed completely in his tale
of other countries close to my heart.

The prophetic strings were bulls' sinews.
But the bulls had grazed on bitter grass.
His throaty voice was like the plaint of a girl
with a hand squeezing her mouth.

The flame of the fire, the flame of the fire, columns
of red trunks and a deafening whoop.
The guest in love tramples the rusty leaves,
a Bengal tiger circling in the crowd.

Drops of blood flow from his prickly moustache,
he's out of it, he's full, he's drunk,
oh, here there are too many crashing tambourines,
too many sweet, fragrant bodies.

Is it for me to watch him in the cigar smoke
where the corks pop, the people shout,
beating out the rhythm of an evil heart
on the white table with an amber mouthpiece;

for me who remembers him in a diamond boat
on the river running away to the Creator,
like a storm of angels and a sweet seduction
with a bloodstained lily in a slender hand?

Girl, what's up with you? He's a rich guest,
get up before him like a comet in the night.
Tear out, tear out his heart and trample it,
his winged heart in his shaggy breast.

Circle wider and wider,
go on, go on, and beckon him,
so the evening floats in the meadows
when the fires, the fires are beyond the woods.

The strings of the bulls are left and right.
Their horns of death and bellowing spell disaster.
They have bitter herbs in their pasture,
prickly thistles, wormwood, goosefoot.

He wants to get up but can't. . . the flint is sharp-toothed,
the sharp-toothed flint like a throaty shout
has penetrated his winged heart
under the menacingly raised velvet paw.

He collapsed on his chest, chink of metal on braid,
no drinking now, no watching,
the waiters bustle around
carrying off the drunken guest.

Gentlemen — it's half past five!
The bill, please, Satan!
The girl laughs and with her slim tongue
licks the blood from the strip of flint.

Nightingales in the cypresses and moon over the lake,
black rock, white rock, much wine have I drunk.
Now the bottle sang to me louder than my heart:
the world is just a beam from a friend's face, all else is his shadow!

I fell in love with the cupbearer not today, not yesterday,
not yesterday and not today drunk from the very morning.
I go, I boast that I have found a triumph:
the world is just a beam from a friend's face, all else is his shadow!

A vagabond and robber, a good for nothing,
I have forgotten forever everything I learned
for a flushed smile and a simple refrain:
the world is just a beam from a friend's face, all else is his shadow!

Now I go among the graves where my friends are lying,
can I not ask the dead about love?
A skull screams from the pit the secret of its grave:
the world is just a beam from a friend's face, all else is his shadow!

Under the moon streams stirred in the smoky lake,
in tall cypresses nightingales fell silent,
just one sang out so loud, the one that had sung nothing:
the world is just a beam from a friend's face, all else is his shadow!

THE LEOPARD

If you don't immediately singe the whiskers
off a killed leopard, its spirit will persecute the hunter.
ABYSSINIAN LORE

The leopard I killed
is up to witchcraft
and sorcery in my room
in the deep silence of the nights.

People come in and go away,
last of all she goes away
for whom the golden darkness
wanders in my veins.

It's late. The mice have squeaked,
the house spirit has coughed
and the leopard I killed
purrs beside my bed.

'A grey-blue mist floats
over the ravines of Dobrobran,
the sun, red as a wound,
floods Dobrobran with light.

The wind chases to the east
the smell of honey and verbena
and the hyenas roar and roar
and bury their noses in the sand.

My brother, my enemy, do you hear
the roars? Sense the smell, see the smoke?
Why then do you breathe
this moist air?

No, my murderer,
you must die in my country
so that I can be born again
into the family of leopards.'

Will I really catch before dawn
his crafty call?
Ah, I did not listen to the advice.
I did not singe his whiskers.

It's too late. The enemy power
has overcome and is close:
suddenly the back of my neck is crushed
as though by a bronze hand.

Palms. . . A terrifying flame from the sky
burns the sands' watering hole.
The Danakil has fallen on a rock
with his flaming spear.

He does not know, does not ask
why my soul is proud,
he just abandons this soul
not knowing where.

I cannot fight back,
I am calm, I stand up.
I will finish my life
by the giraffes' well.

I remember the ancient master craftsmen's prayer:
'Preserve us, O Lord, from those students

who want our poor genius to search out
blasphemously newer and newer revelations.

We can like the direct and honest enemy,
but these ones track our every step.

It delights them that we're struggling to the point
when Peter denies, and Judas betrays.

The limits of our strength are known only to heaven;
who concealed what is weighed up by posterity.

What we will create in the future is in God's power,
but what we have created is with us today.

We greet all the revilers, but we say
no to those who overpraise!

Flattering reproaches and the buzzing praise of rumour
are not required for the shrine of creativity.

It's shameful for you to drug the master with henbane
like a Carthaginian elephant before the war.

A girl dropped a ring
into a well, a well of night.
She stretched her slender fingers
to the cold spring water.

'Well, give me back my ring,
it has a red ruby from Ceylon,
what will the little people, the tritons
and water nymphs do with it?'

The water darkened in the depths,
a commotion and a murmur came:
'We liked your ring
for its warmth of a living body.'

'My betrothed is faint with worry,
he'll plunge his fevered hands
through the water's mirror
and cry hot tears.'

Wet ugly faces of nymphs and tritons
appeared above the surface:
'We liked your ruby
for its human blood.'

'My betrothed lives by one prayer alone,
one prayer alone of love.
If I ask him, he will cut
his veins open with a steel razor.'

'Your ring must have healing powers
if you pray for it so anxiously,
if the magic price you'll pay for it
is a man's love?'

'It's simple, gold is more beautiful
than the body, rubies redder than blood,
until now I have not understood
what love is.'

Early in the morning
the happy herdsman drove
his cows into the shady dales
of Broceliande.

The cows grazed
and he played
a joyous song
on his reed pipe.

Suddenly beyond the branches
he heard a song but not a bird's.
He sees the flame-like bird
with a sweet girl's head.

The song stopped and started
as a baby cries in sleep.
There was a longing in her dark eyes
as in those of eastern captives.

The herdsman is amazed
and looks penetratingly:
'Such a beautiful bird,
yet it groans so heavily.'

Confused, he listened
to her answer:
'There are none like me
on this green earth.

Although a bird-boy
full of wonderful desires
must indeed be born
in Broceliande,

yet wicked fate
will grant us no joy:
think of it, herdsman, I must
die before his birth.

No longer do I love
the sun or the high moon,
no one needs my lips
nor my pale cheeks.

But what I most regret,
though I treasure it most,
is that the bird-boy too
will suffer sadness.

He'll soar over the meadow,
settle on these elms
and call his girlfriend
who doesn't yet exist.

Herdsman, you may be rough
but I can cope with it.
Come close and kiss my lips
and delicate neck.

You are young, will want to marry,
you will have children too
and the memory of the bird-girl
will fly to other centuries.'

The herdsman breathes in the smell
of skin, warmed by the sun,
hears the golden bracelets
tinkling on the bird's feet.

Now he is beside himself,
doesn't know what he is doing.
His sunburnt knees
thrust on the red feathers.

The bird groaned only once,
just once did she groan,
and in her breast her heart
suddenly stopped beating.

She won't come back to life,
her eyes have turned dark
and over her the herdsman
plays sad songs on his pipe.

The grey mists arise
with the evening cool,
and he drives his herd
home from Broceliande.

An old vagabond in Addis Ababa,
having subjugated many tribes,
sent me a black spear-carrier
with a greeting composed of my poems.
A lieutenant who took gunboats
under fire of enemy batteries
read me my poems from memory
all night on the southern sea.
A man who shot the emperor's
ambassador among a crowd of people
came to shake my hand
to thank me for my poems.

Many of those, strong, wicked and joyful
who've killed elephants and men,
who've almost died from thirst in the desert,
frozen on the edge of the eternal ice,
true to our planet,
strong, joyful and wicked,
carry my books in their saddlebags,
read them in the palm grove,
and forget them as the ship sinks.

I do not insult them with neurasthenia,
don't demean them with soulfulness,
I won't bore them with many-layered hints
at the contents of a half-consumed egg;
but when bullets whistle around,
when waves break the bows,
I will teach them how not to fear,
not to fear and to do what has to be done.
And when a woman with a beautiful face —
uniquely dear in the universe —

says: 'I don't love you',
I will teach them how to smile
and leave and never come back.
And when their last hour comes,
an even, red mist will cover their gazes:
I will teach them to remember at once
all this cruel, sweet life,
all this familiar, strange land,
and having appeared before the face of God
with simple and wise words
to wait calmly for His judgement.

It was a gold night,
a gold night but moonless.
He ran, ran across the plain,
fell on his knees, raised himself,
rushed about like a shot hare,
and hot tears streamed
down his cheeks, pitted and furrowed,
down his he-goat old man's chin.
And after him ran his children,
and after him ran his grandchildren,
and in the tent of unbleached canvas
the forsaken great-grandchild squealed.

'Come back,' the children cried to him,
and the grandchildren pressed their palms together.
'Nothing bad has happened,
the sheep have not eaten the euphorbia,
the rain has not flooded the sacred fire,
nor has the shaggy lion or the cruel Zend
come to our tent.'

A steep black slope loomed in front of him,
the old man did not see the slope in the dark,
he crashed in a bone-jarring fall
that almost knocked the soul from him.
And then he still tried to crawl
but the children had already caught him
and the grandchildren held him by the sleeves,
and these were the words he said to them:

'Woe! Woe! Fear — the noose and the pit
for those born on earth,
because the black one gazes

from the sky with so many eyes
and spies out his secrets.
This night I went to sleep as usual,
rolled up in my hide, face to the ground,
I dreamed of a fine cow
with a swollen udder,
I crawled under her like a grass-snake
to revive myself with fresh milk
when suddenly she kicked me,
I turned over and woke up:
I was without my skin, face to the sky.
It was good that a skunk had only
burnt out my right eye with its foul juice,
otherwise if I had looked with both eyes
I would have been left dead there.
Woe! Woe! Fear – the noose and the pit
for those born on earth.'

The children lowered their gazes to the ground,
the grandchildren hid their faces with their elbows,
everyone waited in silence for the eldest son
with the grey beard to speak
and these were the words he said:

'All my life nothing bad
has happened to me, and my heart
beats in the belief that nothing bad
will happen to me in the future.
With both eyes I want to see
who it is that wanders in the sky.'

He spoke and immediately lay on the ground,
not face down but on his back,
everyone stood and held their breath.
They listened and waited for a long time.
Then trembling with fear the old man asked:

'What do you see?' But his son
with the grey beard gave no answer.
And when his brothers leant over him
they saw that he wasn't breathing,
that his face was darker than bronze,
distorted by the hands of death.

Ah, the women's voices,
how the children cried and howled,
the old man plucked his beard, hoarsely
calling out terrible curses.
Then eight brothers – strong men – jumped
to their feet, seized their bows,
'Let's shoot,' they said, 'at the sky,
and we'll shoot down the one who wanders there . . .
Why has this disaster come on us?'
But the dead man's widow screamed:
'Let revenge be mine, not yours!
I want to see his face,
to tear out his throat with my teeth
and claw out his eyes.'

She screamed and crashed on the ground,
but screwing up her eyes, long
whispered curses to herself,
tore at her breast and bit her fingers.
Finally she looked up, grinned
and cuckooed forth like a cuckoo:

'Lin, why are you going to the lake? Linoya,
is the antelope liver good?
Children, the pitcher's beak is broken,
I'll get you! Father, get up quickly,
do you see, the Zends with mistletoe twigs
are dragging the reed baskets away,
they're going off to trade, not to fight.

How many fires there are here, how many people!
The whole tribe has gathered . . . a wonderful holiday!'

The old man began to calm down,
to touch the bumps on his knees,
the children put down their bows,
the grandchildren grew bolder, even smiled.
But when the woman who was lying down jumped
to her feet, then everyone turned green,
everyone sweated with fear.
Black, but with white eyes,
she rushed around furiously wailing:
'Woe! Woe! Fear – the noose and the pit!
Where am I? What's happening to me? The red swan
is chasing after me. The three-headed dragon
steals up . . . Go away beasts, beasts!
Cancer, don't touch! Flee from Capricorn!'

And when still with the same wailing,
with the wailing of a dog out of its mind,
she rushed up the crest of the hill to the abyss,
nobody ran after her in pursuit.

The people returned to the tents confused,
sat around on the cliffs and were fearful.
The time was approaching midnight. The hyena
howled and was suddenly quiet.
And the people said: 'He who is in the sky,
a god or a beast, probably wants a sacrifice.
We must bring him a little body,
a chaste virgin,
one whom no man to this day
has ever looked on with desire.
Gar is dead. Garaya has gone out of her mind.
Their daughter is only eight springs old,
perhaps she'll be all right.'

The women ran off swiftly
and dragged out young Garra.
The old man raised the flint axe,
and thought: 'It's better to smash her temple
before she looks at the sky.'
She's his grandchild after all and he pities her.
But the others did not let him and said:
'What sort of sacrifice is one with a smashed temple?'

They placed the little girl on a rock,
a flat, black rock on which
the holy flame had burned until
it went out in the time of confusion.
They placed her there and turned away their faces.
They waited for her to die
so they could go to sleep before the sun came up.

Only the little girl did not die.
She looked up, then to the right
where her brothers were standing,
then up again. She wanted to jump off the rock.
The old man did not let her, and called out:
'What do you see?'
She answered angrily:
'I don't see anything. Only the sky,
curved, black, empty
and there are fires everywhere in the sky
like flowers in a marsh in spring.'
The old man thought for a moment and said
'Look again' and Garra looked at the sky
for a long, long time.
'Now,' she said, 'it's not little flowers,
it is just gold fingers
showing us the plain
and the sea and the mountains of the Zends,
showing what happened,
what is happening, and what will happen.'

The people listened in wonder:
it was not just children, not even men
had spoken like that up till then,
and Garra's cheeks flamed,
her eyes shone with sparks, her lips were crimson,
her arms were raised to the sky
as though she wanted to fly up there.
And she sang out so surprisingly
like the wind in a reed thicket,
the wind from the hills of Iran on the Euphrates.

Mella was eighteen springs old
but she had never known a man,
she fell down alongside Garra,
looked and sang out.
And after Mella, Akha, and after Akha,
Urr, her bridegroom, and the whole tribe
lay and sang, sang, sang
like skylarks on a hot midday,
or frogs on a troubled evening.

Only the old man went aside,
pressing his fists to his ears,
and tear flowed after tear from his one eye.
He cried for his fall from the slope,
for the bumps on his knees, for Gar
and his widow, and for the times when people
looked at the plain where their flocks grazed,
at the water where their sails skimmed,
at the grass where their children played,
but not at the black sky where sparkle
the unattainable, alien stars.

1921

Late Poems

Dawn has not broken yet,
it's neither night nor morning,
the crow under my window,
half-asleep, stirs its wing
and star after star in the sky
melts away for ever.

This is the hour when I can do everything:
penetrate my helpless enemy in thought
or leap onto his chest
as a maned nightmare.
Or enter into the bedroom of a girl
to whom only an angel knew the way,
and cut oblivion with a ray of light,
to impress my features
on her sleepy memory
as a symbol of the highest beauty.

But it's quiet in the world, so quiet
that the cautious step of the night beast,
the flight of the owl, nomad of the heights
can be perceived.
Somewhere the ocean dances
and above it a whitish mist has risen
like smoke from the pipe of a sailor
whose corpse is barely visible in the sand.
A pre-dawn breeze
streams, joyful and cruel,
as strangely joyful and cruel
as I — it's just my fate.

An alien life — for what?
Will I drink mine to the dregs?

Will I understand with all my will
the uniqueness of a single earthly stem?
You who sleep round me,
you, not meeting the day,
because I had mercy on you
and burnt my hour in solitude,
allow me to meet
tomorrow's darkness alone.

TO ***

If you meet me, you'll not recognize me!
You hear my name – you'll hardly remember!
I talked to you only once,
once only kissed your hands.

But I swear that you will be mine
even if you love another,
even if for long years
you don't succeed in meeting me!

I swear to you by the white church
that we saw together at dawn,
in this church a seraph with a fiery look
married us invisibly.

I swear to you by those dreams
that I see now every night,
and by my great anguish
for you in the great desert,

in that desert where the hills rose
like your young breasts,
and the sunsets flamed in the sky
like your bloodied lips.

'THE WHITE WILLOW. . .'

The white willow loomed. At its top
the rooks ruffled their wings,
the clouds, like sheep, grazed
in the blue, blue valley of the sky.

And you with a submissive look
said: 'I'm in love with you.'
The grass was all around, like the sea,
the time was after noon.

I kissed the flames of summer —
the shadow of grass was on your pink cheeks,
the fragrant festival of light
in your bronzed curls.

You seemed to me as desirable
as a fabled country,
some promised land
of rapture, wine and song.

I

The whole sky is lit up
with the silver of cold dawn.
The ship is making its way
between Stambul and Scutari.
The little boats dance like dolphins
and how joyously salty
are your young lips
from the fresh, salt waves.
Look, like a lion's mane
three huge cliffs arise —
they are the Prince's Islands
coming out of the blue haze.
There are shafts of amber light in the sea
and a forest of blood-red coral,
or is it the pink dawn
come down from the skies that has drowned?
No, it is simply a huge swarm
of red jelly-fish,
so said the Frenchman,
who was courting you
Look, he's coming to you again
and kissing your hand. . .
But can I be jealous —
I who love too much?
You see, all night while you were sleeping,
I couldn't sleep a wink,
all the time I watched how miraculously white
and like a royal cup was your breast.
We are sailing down the old route
of the joyful, migrating birds;

sailing in reality not in dreams
to the golden land of fables.

II

The old port of Athens
Piraeus rose above us
in a muddled network of masts and rigging
and houses running down from the heights.
Pant, you stubborn steam train!
Jingle and squeak, coach!
At last it's given to us to be there
under long familiar skies.
The July rain covers
your veil with pearls,
the distance hurls the slender outline
of olive groves to meet us.
We are in Athens. We hasten
over the paths and cliffs:
beyond the poplar fence rose
a tall marble temple,
the temple to Pallas Athene. Before this
you were not completely mine.
Throw a gold coin into the rock-cleft
and you'll be as strong as I am.
You'll understand that nothing is terrible
and also nothing is sad,
and in your soul will flare the light
of the most free of God's comets.
But we will be one together
in this quiet evening hour,
and the goddess with the long spear
will marry us for glory.

The seagulls beckon us to Port Said,
the wind brought the heat from the desert.
Crete was on the right
and dear Rhodes on the left.
Here is the broad Lesseps mole,
the blinding houses.
There is a hubbub like a swarm of bees,
the harbour is bustling.
We have important business here —
without it our day would be empty —
to sit on the hotel terrace
and order baked langouste.
There is nothing in the world more delicious
than pink lobster tails,
with the light spice of Rhine wine poured on them.
The evening is warm. The murmur stills
and the houses are transparent shadows.
You and I walk alone
through the silent squares.
Master of your hand,
I'll tell you a story
about a fate as miraculous as a dream,
about your fate and mine.
I remember that in the past
there was a black moon, black as hell:
we parted and I beckoned
you back with poems alone.
But then you remember — there are no
slender palms around and the fountain does not play;
and no steamer waits for us
to take us further south.
An evil night in Petersburg,
I am alone with pen in hand,

and no one can help
my perpetual ache, my longing.
The pages grieve with poems
which perhaps you won't read. . .
Why did you believe
in people's boring lies?
I love, immortally love
all that sang in your words,
and I mourn, mortally mourn
for the petals of your lips.
The poison of love and shame of dreaming!
I am powerless, I don't know —
What is a dream? Are you my cruel
or my tender one?

1920

In the morning of my unsure memory
I recall a many-coloured meadow,
where ruled a haughty
turkey, adored by me.

He was malicious and free,
his beak crimson as fire
and he was sharply scornful
of my four years.

Neither chocolate, nor caramels,
nor pineapple juice
could comfort me
in the realization of my shame.

Once more came disaster
and shame and grief of childhood years,
you, my adored one, cruel girl
answer me proudly: 'No!'

But all passes in this unsteady life —
love will pass, sadness too,
and I will remember you with a smile
as I remember the turkey.

1920

No, nothing has changed
in poor and simple nature,
but everything miraculously was lit
by inexpressible beauty.

This must be how people's
powerless flesh will appear
when the Lord summons it on Judgement Day
out of the measureless darkness.

You should know, my proud, tender friend,
that with you, with you alone,
my red-head, white as a swan,
I became myself for a moment.

You smiled, my darling,
and you yourself couldn't grasp
how radiant you are
and what gloom has thickened round you.

1920

The poet is lazy, although the swan
day does not fade in his soul,
although he is too lazy to scatter his poems
like diamonds, sapphires and rubies.

His law is tirelessly like a miser
to store in his memory the smiles
of his beloved woman, green-eyed looks
and the smooth of the sky.

To doze like Tancred with Armida,
like Achilles by the ships,
cherishing childish grievances
against uninformed people.

So, be blessed therefore,
cruel words of love,
giving birth to momentary fire
in blood that flows with nectar.

He rose. Swift Pegasus soared,
his mane in the wind, and he flies,
and poems scatter like sparks
from under the flashing hooves.

1920

'YOU AND I ARE BOUND...'

You and I are bound together by the same chain
but I am composed and compose.
I give up my living soul
to fantastical splendour.
And you look distrustfully
at the sun, at me, at everyone.
To your maidenlike meekness
the universe is an empty shell.
But still you argue, and your gaze is stern,
and more unsuccessful every day
are your intricate excuses
for not being alone with me.

1920

'DON'T CALL THE BLIND MUSIC'

Don't call the blind music
of my love enchanting.

Words float on the shadows of evening.

The heart is more aflame, more gold
on the distant star Venus.
On Venus, ah, on Venus,
the trees have blue leaves.

Everywhere there are free, ringing waters,
rivers, geysers, waterfalls
chorus at midday the song of freedom,
and at night they burn like ikon-lamps.

On Venus, ah, on Venus,
there are no hurtful or harsh words.
The angels on Venus speak
a language of vowels only.

If they say 'e-a' and 'a-i'
it is a joyful promise.
'U-o', 'a-o' are a golden memory
of ancient paradise.

On Venus, ah, on Venus
there is no sharp or choking death.
Those who die on Venus
are turned into airy steam.

The golden smoke drifts
in the blue, blue evening tree-tops,
or like joyous pilgrims
visits those who are still alive.

1921

'I PLAYED A JOKE ON MYSELF'

I played a joke on myself
and tricked myself
when I thought that there was something
in the world apart from you.

Pure white, in a white garment
like an ancient goddess's tunic,
you hold the crystal ball
in your translucent, slender fingers.

All the oceans, all the mountains,
archangels, people, flowers —
were reflected in the crystal
of your transparent maiden's eyes.

How strange it is to think that there is
anything in the world apart from you,
and that I myself am not only a night's
sleepless song about you.

But there's a light from behind your shoulders,
such a blinding light.
There tall flames soar,
like two golden wings.

1921

'I CAME BACK'

I came back
after so many years,
but I am an exile
and they are watching me.

'I waited for you
all those long days.
My love knows
no distance.'

My life went by
in foreign lands.
I never noticed
how they stole it from me.

'My life
was sweet.
I waited for you,
dreamed of you.'

Death is in my home
and in your home.
But death is nothing
if we are together.

1921

Notes

BY MICHAEL BASKER

It is a measure of Gumilyov's almost unrivalled popularity among present-day Russian readers of poetry that there have been more than 40 editions of his selected verse since his rehabilitation in 1986. Only two have partially superseded the long-serving American edition described in Richard McKane's Preface: these are Gumilyov's *Stikhotvoreniya i poemy*, ed. M. D. El'zon, in the prestigious 'Poet's Library' series (Leningrad, 1988); and a 3-volume 'Works', ed. N. A. Bogomolov et al. (*Sochineniya*, Moscow, 1991). But the definitive text is set to become a new 10-volume Academy edition, of which only Volumes 1 and 2 have so far appeared: N. S. Gumilyov, *Polnoe sobranie sochinenii*, ed. Iu. V. Zobnin et al., text and commentary by M. Basker et al., Moscow, 1998–. For the reader of Russian, this contains extensive notes on each poem. For a select bibliography of works about Gumilyov, in Russian and English, see M. Basker's entry on Gumilyov in *Reference Guide to Russian Literature*, ed. N. Cornwell (London: Fitzroy Dearborn, 1998).

IN THE HEAVENS One of several stellar poems by Gumilyov, who in his Acmeist manifesto was nevertheless to reject Symbolist speculation on 'the unknowable' with the observation that 'all the beauty, all the sacred significance of the stars is that they are infinitely far from the earth'. An earlier version of this piece, revised by Gumilyov in 1918, contained echoes of poems by the most gifted Symbolist, Alexander Blok.

THOUGHTS The rhetorical structure of this poem, and the bitter theme of an implacable, vengeful fate, evoke the work of Russia's leading Romantic, Mikhail Lermontov (1814–41), with whose ill-starred lot a parallel is implied. The notion of poetry as an accursed activity is frequent in early Gumilyov, and lines 13ff. have been taken by at least one critic as prescient of his untimely end.

REJECTION The poem was written after Akhmatova-Gorenko turned down a proposal of marriage which Gumilyov made to her in Sebastopol in summer 1907, having travelled from Paris to see her. Akhmatova later recalled that they stood in silence by the sea shore, on which a dead dolphin had been washed up. Yet it is typical of Gumilyov that the autobiographical element is mediated through literature: dolphins, which passed from classical mythology to early Christianity as symbols of God's preserving power, and the vehicles by which the souls of the shipwrecked were transported to heaven, frequently occur in Russian Symbolist poetry. Gumilyov's poem may be a re-working of Andrey Bely's 'Evening Excursion'.

HYENA The themes of Ancient Egypt and Cleopatra were no less popular in turn-of-the-century Russia than in Western Europe. The decadent eroticism of Gumilyov's several variations on the Cleopatran theme seems invariably connected with nocturnal motifs of dream and the occult (here, necromancy and reincarnation).

JAGUAR Originally entitled 'Betrayal' — which Akhmatova took to refer to the relationship with her: a significance which Gumilyov himself had supposedly forgotten when he retitled and revised the poem in 1918. Yet 'Betrayal' might equally convey the young Gumilyov's attitude to Symbolism, for the 'White Bride' (here turned predatory *femme fatale*) is of course a Symbolist archetype.

TERROR Gumilyov's choice of imagery has been variously traced to Poe, Gautier, and the initiation ceremonies of pre-Christian mystery cults.

THE GARDENS OF MY SOUL Gumilyov told the beautiful future poet Vera Yevgenevna Arens (1890–1962) that this poem, less gloomy than many of the period, was dedicated to her. Again he draws on the imagery both of ancient mystery cults (Dionysus, Cybele) and of the contemporary Symbolism which may have inspired that interest: in particular, here, on the poetry of Konstantin Balmont (whose mellifluous imprecision Gumilyov shifts in the direction of the plastic-sculptural), and perhaps the ornate paintings of Gustave Moreau, which he much admired as a student in Paris.

GIRAFFE The most famous of Gumilyov's early poems, notable for its dual-planed combination of exotic subject-matter with the psychological realism of an acutely observed humdrum present, and for its neat 'metapoetic' depiction of the creation of a poem within a poem. 'Giraffe' was a favourite target of parodists, who enthusiastically mimicked its distinctive five-foot amphibrachic metre; while critics and memoirists not infrequently likened the poet himself to an 'elegant giraffe'.

ll. 13–14: one admittedly far from 'happy' 'tale of mysterious lands', concerning an unresponsive 'black maiden' and passionate 'young hero', is Gumilyov's exotic short story 'Princess Zara'. Closely related to 'Giraffe' in time of composition, thematics and psychological circumstance, this is another elaborately disguised refraction of Gumilyov's tormented relationship with his bride-to-be, Akhmatova.

LAKE CHAD First published together with 'Giraffe' (several motifs of which are here intriguingly inverted) as the third poem of a cycle also entitled 'Lake Chad'. The poems were written in Paris towards the end of 1907, before Gumilyov had experienced what he later termed the 'real Africa'.

BARBARIANS Gumilyov regarded this poem as a new departure. He claimed he was consciously following the example of the French Parnassian, Leconte de Lisle, in 'introducing realistic description into the most fantastic subject matter' as a means of escaping the Symbolist imprecision of Blok. There is a striking parallel to the Greek poet, who lived in Alexandria, Constantine Cavafy (1863–1933). His 1904 poem 'Waiting for the Barbarians' also has the barbarians turn away. It finishes: 'Now what's going to happen to us without barbarians? / Those people were a kind of solution.' [Translated by Edmund Keeley and Philip Sherrard]

CHRIST The poem clearly draws on the account of Jesus's encounter with his first disciples in *Matthew* 4, and should probably be understood as a deliberate rejoinder to the sombre image of the 'Russian Christ', much celebrated by Dostoyevsky and the Symbolists. This stems in particular from a Crimean War poem by Fyodor Tyutchev (1803–73), which portrays a humiliated Christ, worn down by the burden of the Cross, wandering the breadth of the meagre, suffering, native land. In form and intonation Gumilyov's poem also recalls the famous poem about the holy wanderer 'Vlas' by the great 19th-century civic poet Nekrasov (1821–78), and marks an important stage in his elaboration of the theme of life itself as a spiritual 'wandering' or pilgrimage (even his Christ is a 'searcher').

The use of 'pink' in this and several poems of the period ('Pink Pearl' was also a separate section of Gumilyov's third book of verse) probably derives from alchemical symbolism, and appears to signify the new dawn of spiritual development or regeneration, generally connected with the acquisition of esoteric wisdom.

MARQUIS DE KARABAS The poem was written in Novgorod Province in early spring, 1910, on the small country estate of Gumilyov's friend, the minor prose writer Sergey Auslender. The 'clever cat' of stanza 8 is familiar to Russian readers as the teller of fairy tales from the Introduction to Pushkin's *Ruslan and Lyudmila*, and suggests the possibility of a reading in terms of the artist and his inspiration; while the landscape (despite the use of Perrault's fairy tale) is itself indicative of an experiment by Gumilyov in the spirit of Pushkinian realism.

JOURNEY TO CHINA Sergey Sudeykin (1882–1946) belonged to the 'World of Art' group, and was closely associated with the poet Mikhail Kuzmin (1872–1936). The poem may be connected with his painting 'Voyage to Cythera' which Gumilyov owned. Certainly 'Journey to China' seems to mark a growing complexity and sophistication in Gumilyov's poetry around 1910. It alludes (with undoubted autobiographical feeling) to Pushkin seeking to flee Russia for 'distant China' on the eve of marriage, and polemicizes with the death-obsessed *ennui* of Baudelaire's symbolistic 'Le Voyage', as well as referring openly to Rabelais – the Renaissance

French author whose reputation as grand occultist magician and one of the 'True Adepts' of history is as important to his function in the poem as the text of his writings. The crux of the poem seems to be that the redemption of the fallen Adam (cf. the Biblical overtones of the first stanzas) is possible here on earth, through a spiritual journey toward altered perception, the acquisition of a child-like, 'physiological' wisdom (as Gumilyov characterized the lesson of Rabelais in his Acmeist manifesto) which enables a liberating acceptance of all, including death, that life may (or may not) offer. By a complex bilingual pun involving the Biblical Cain and Rabelais' native Chinon, 'China' might in this respect be identified with the point of departure, something deeply akin to T. S. Eliot's 'the end of all our exploring/Will be to arrive where we started /And know the place for the first time.'

LAKES The darkness closes in again (in a poem written before 'Journey to China', but placed after it in the final edition of *Pearls*), although here, too, Gumilyov ends with an acceptance of this earth, rather than a Symbolist dream world.

RENDEZVOUS May have been addressed to the young artist Nadezhda Voitinskaya, who in 1909 made a lithographic portrait of Gumilyov (reproduced on the cover), and recalled posing in return, dressed in some strange garment, for this 'poetic portrait'. She afterwards recollected: 'he always called me his Lady. There was not an iota of real passion on his part or mine, but he acted out adoration and passion. It was purest theatre.' Akhmatova, however, maintained the poem was dedicated to Lydia Arens (a sister of Vera: see note to 'The Gardens of My Soul'), with whom Gumilyov had a brief but seemingly passionate affair.

'DO YOU REMEMBER THE PALACE. . .' This poem was written only shortly before Gumilyov's wedding to Akhmatova in April 1910, and its wistful, fairy-tale nostalgia evidently conceals acute biographical pain at the course of their love. Stanzas 1 and 3 evoke the artificial ruin of the 'Turkish Tower' at Tsarskoye Selo, where the two used to meet, and stanza 2 an episode when they had watched, unobserved, a cuirassier trying to rein in his rearing horse.

PARROT Gumilyov kept a caged parrot at Tsarskoye Selo; and 'the magician' (line 2) may be a metaphor for the poet. The 'ugly secret' (line 14) may thus reflect not only on Symbolist-incantatory verse, but more generally on the opposition of poetic creation to life – all the more so in that the Faustian image of the constricting cell is taken up in some of the immediately following poems. But an alternative reading might find in this piece a reflection on the spirit of colonialism.

THIS HAPPENED OFTEN The Romantic theme of love as battle was well represented in Russian poetry by Lermontov, Tyutchev and Nekrasov. Akhmatova believed the poem referred to her.

PRAYER The poem appears to combine ancient solar myth with imagery derived from Nietzsche's *Thus Spoke Zarathustra* (cf. 'I love him who justifies the men of the future and redeems the men of the past: for he wants to perish by the men of the present'). The latter was avidly read (in Russian translation) by the young Gumilyov, and powerfully influenced the Russian turn-of-the-century mentality. A similar approach to past and future in the context of cultural preservation is found in the mature Mandelstam.

CAPTAINS I The first part of a four-poem cycle. It was written in June 1909 at the Black Sea home of the poet Maximilian Voloshin, at a time when the poet E. I. Dmitriyeva, with whom Gumilyov had travelled there, had plainly begun to transfer her affections to Voloshin. A bizarre pretence on the part of Voloshin and Dmitriyeva subsequently culminated in Gumilyov's inconclusive duel with Voloshin that November.

The popular appeal of 'Captains I' (including, it would seem, for young communists during the Stalinist years of Gumilyov's strict proscription) did much to inculcate the conception of Gumilyov as poet-warrior, and was in Akhmatova's view a serious obstacle to deeper appreciation of his work. The remaining poems of the cycle nevertheless have more to do with mental than geographical horizons, and (especially in the light of the final lighthouse-refuge) suggest that even this piece may be read metaphorically, as a bravado variant on the theme of the wanderer.

TO A GIRL The 'Turgenev-like' heroine of this poem (and of the following item, 'Doubt') was Masha (Mariya Aleksandrovna) Kuzmina-Karavayeva (1888–1911), the daughter of Gumilyov's maternal cousin. Tall, slender and blonde, Masha became the object of his seemingly intense platonic attachment – coloured, however, by his literary awareness of Byronic and Lermontovian precedent, and of the mystical rituals of courtly love – in the environs of his newly discovered family home at Slepnyovo during the summer of 1911. (Akhmatova had gone alone to Paris.) Masha was to die of consumption at the year's end.

The 'crazy hunter' of the last stanza may be another instance of Gumilyov's Nietzschean imagery.

FRAGMENT The final exclamation is a wryly ironic indication that the clash of values between religious morality and cultural creativity remains unresolved. The figure of Dante's Beatrice, seemingly straddling the two 'traditions', introduces the additional consideration of the nature and 'place' of love.

CONSTANTINOPLE The Acmeist Gumilyov here introduces concrete detail (stanza 3) and psychological observation into a Romantic theme – that of the Muslim woman drowned for love, which may be traced to Byron's *Giaour* (the prose introduction) and Pushkin's *Fountain of Bakhchisaray*

(again two heroines), with more recent Russian precedents in the poetry of
Afanasy Fet (1820–92) and Mirra Lokhvitskaya (1869–1905).

MODERNITY Gumilyov's fondness for *The Iliad* – which he took to the front
during the war, and had confiscated from him in prison during his last days
– is well attested, but the sentiment of these opening lines bears closer
comparison to Mallarmé's famous 'Brise marine': 'La chair est triste, hélas,
et j'ai lu tous les livres. . .' The closing reference to the pastoral figures
of Daphnis and Chloe is an allusion to the youthful Gumilyov and
Akhmatova at Tsarskoye Selo, echoed by Akhmatova in her 1912 poem
'I was returning home from school' (see Epilogue to this book).

FROM A DRAGON'S LAIR Written within a year of Gumilyov's wedding.
Akhmatova had lived with her mother, principally in Kiev, following her
parents' separation in 1905, and the poem draws on Ukrainian demonology,
including the legend of Viy used by Nikolay Gogol. The 'Bald Mountain'
is known as a place of witches' sabbaths near Nikolskaya Slobodka in
Chernigov Province, where the Gumilyovs were married. The word for
'bog' in the final stanza, however (a recurrent *topos* of Gumilyov's poetry;
cf. also the recurrence in stanza 2 of the theme of the drowning woman from
'Constantinople', and that of the wounded bird in stanza 4 from 'Flowers
don't live in my home. . .') is a dialectism restricted to Tver Province in
Northern Russia, site of the Gumilyov family home at Slepnyovo.

Akhmatova more than once hauntingly (hauntedly) invoked this poem,
and hence the shade of Gumilyov, many years after his death (see, for
instance, her 'Incantation' of 1936). It was also an apparent subtext of one
of Mandelstam's very last poems, 'Some wife searches':

> Some wife, I don't know whose, searches
> the streets of the monster Kiev for her husband.
> And on her waxen cheeks
> not one tear drop has streaked. . .

[Translated by Richard and Elizabeth McKane: from Osip Mandelstam,
The Voronezh Notebooks]

I BELIEVED, I THOUGHT Sergey Makovsky (1877–1962): art critic and editor
of the journal *Apollo*, for which Gumilyov became chief critic and editor of
the poetry section; in emigration in later years, author of extensive
memoirs of Gumilyov and other Silver Age figures. Stanza 2 echoes the
temporal conception of 'Prayer'. It has been suggested that the last two
stanzas owe something to Théophile Gautier's poem 'Chinoiserie'.

POISONED As so often where Gumilyov takes the theme of a woman bringing
death to a man, Akhmatova believed that this poem was about her.

BY THE FIRE Gumilyov wrote this poem on his way to Africa in autumn 1910,
and immediately posted it to Akhmatova. The title might initiate an ironic

contrast with the domestic contentment of Pushkin's 'Winter Road'. It seems likely that Akhmatova's 'Grey-Eyed King' of December 1910 was conceived in part as a poetic rejoinder.

THE RAGAMUFFIN This appears to be a polemical reworking of the recent 'Russian' subject matter of the leading Symbolists, Alexander Blok and, especially, Andrey Bely, in which Gumilyov is also attempting a fresh approach to his own theme of the wanderer.

VENICE One of a series of poems on Italian cities which were the result of a visit to Italy with Akhmatova in summer 1912. Here Gumilyov borrows polemically from Blok's poems on Venice (1909) to offer a less introspective, less gloomily portentous, and, paradoxically, more enigmatically provisional picture of the city as cultural symbol and physical presence.

CONVERSATION Georgy Ivanov (1894–1958): close younger associate of Gumilyov and partisan supporter of Acmeism. Editor of several posthumous volumes of Gumilyov's work, author of notoriously unreliable memoirs of Gumilyov and the Silver Age – and one of the very best poets of the Russian emigration.

In treating the dialogue of body and soul, here and elsewhere, Gumilyov typically attempts to introduce original content into a traditional framework. It has been suggested that the frequenter of *cafés chantants* may represent Ivanov, who echoed motifs from 'Conversation' in several later poems.

FIVE-FOOT IAMBICS Mikhail Lozinsky (1886–1955): poet and subsequently celebrated translator of Shakespeare and of Dante's *Divine Comedy*, Gumilyov's close friend and editorial advisor. After discussing 'autobiographical iambics' with Gumilyov in the light of this poem, Lozinsky wrote and dedicated to him his own autobiographical iambic pentameters – a splendid piece entitled 'Precious Stones', from his 1916 collection *Mountain Stream*. Stanza 2 – Don Juan, Sinbad and the Wandering Jew had all appeared in Gumilyov's earlier verse, and confirm the profoundly autobiographical nature of this poem; the conveniently named Donna Anna is the poem's first allusion to Akhmatova, who again recognized herself as the poem's female persona. Stanza 3 – some of the pictures Gumilyov brought back from Abyssinia are now in the St Petersburg Museum of Anthropology and Ethnography. On his hunting exploits, see note to 'The Leopard', below. Stanza 5 – the story of Prince Nal (or Nala) and his beautiful bride Damayanti is from the Hindu epic *The Mahabharata*, rendered into Russian (from Rückert's German) by the Romantic poet and translator V. A. Zhukovsky (1783–1852). Nala, possessed by a demon, in fact gambles away not Damayanti but his kingdom. Stanzas 8–14 were substituted in 1915 for the overtly Masonic conclusion of a first, 1912 version. Stanza 8 – the stifling, 'apocalyptic' heat of summer

1914 is also described in Akhmatova's poem 'July 1914'. (Compare, too, the opening of Akhmatova's 'That August. . .' in the Epilogue to this book.) Stanza 11 – Gumilyov volunteered within days of Germany's declaration of war against Russia on 18 July 1914. He was in uniform by 5 August, and saw active combat by mid-October (see note to 'The Advance'). Stanza 12 contains a reformulation of lines from Lermontov's famous poem 'I come out alone onto the road'; stanza 13 incorporates words from the Russian Orthodox prayer 'My soul magnifies the Lord'. The closing image of stanza 14 echoes both Gumilyov's earlier poem on the Don Juan theme, and Pushkin's 'Monastery on Mt Kazbek'.

JUDITH The poem is based on the Apocryphal *Book of Judith*, which tells of the beautiful widow who seduced Holofernes, general of Nebuchadnezzar's invading army, to behead him in his tent with his own sword. This story was also used in a poem of the same time by Mandelstam, under the unlikely title of 'Football'. The shared theme doubtless reflects a private literary game, all the more so in that Mandelstam's Judith is known to represent a beautiful, unnamed habitué of the 'Stray Dog' artistic cabaret in St Petersburg: his poem's phonetic structure strongly suggests that his prototypes were in fact Akhmatova and Gumilyov. Salome and John the Baptist were a popular subject of Silver Age Russian poets, inspired primarily by Oscar Wilde's *Salomé*. Gumilyov's Salome should probably be identified with another of the Stray Dog's famous 'beauties', but his concluding lines also involve a further polemical re-working of Blok's 'Venice'. The recurrence of the motif of the severed head in other poems by Gumilyov and his colleagues (see below: 'Dream', 'Second Canto' and 'The Tram that Lost its Way') has prompted some interesting psycho-analytical commentary, scarcely consonant with Gumilyov's image of manly warrior. There are several references to 'headlessness' in Akhmatova, including the decapitation of Madame de Lamballe in *Poem Without a Hero* and the epigraphs from Keats's *Isabella (The Pot of Basil)* to 'The Sweet-briar in Bloom', and from Baudelaire's 'Une Martyre' to 'Cinque'. The Baudelaire poem had been translated by Gumilyov, to whom the epigraph might have included a covert allusion.

STANZAS Gumilyov appears to conflate the islands of Patmos, where St John wrote the *Revelation*, and Paxos, where, according to Plutarch, a voice was heard calling that the great god Pan was dead. The poetic justification is the association in Christian legend of the death of Pan with the birth of Christ.

BIRD Ganymede, 'the most beautiful youth in the world' according to *The Iliad*, was carried off by Zeus in the guise of an eagle. The story is retold, e.g. by Ovid in *Metamorphoses*, but perhaps Gumilyov's immediate source was Dante, who identifies with Ganymede in the dream-vision of an abducting eagle that proves, on waking, to have been no predatory Zeus, but St Lucy, bearing him up to the Gate of Purgatory (*Purgatory*, ix). Certainly the speculative combination of classical and Christian imagery which pervades this poem is a common feature of *Quiver*.

THE SUN OF THE SPIRIT See note on 'The Advance', below.

MEDIAEVAL Written during convalescence from sickness in a Petrograd military hospital in spring 1915, and probably addressed to A. L. Benois, an architect's daughter who worked there as a nurse. The theme of the mediaeval cathedral reflects Gumilyov's interest in Freemasonry, which he shared with Mandelstam and Lozinsky, and is implicit in the Acmeist notions of the poet-craftsman and Guild of Poets. The mystical goal of Esoteric Freemasonry can be represented as the construction of a temple of wisdom, symbolizing the attainment of the individual – and hence mankind – to moral and spiritual perfection in God. The stages of the initiate's progression toward the perfection of Grand Master (in some versions, Christ Himself) are mirrored in a hierarchical view of the human community. This is treated here with an arcane humour (the pretext for amorous indulgence beneath Genevieve's broad cloak for those less spiritually advanced in the Masonic quest), typical of the Acmeists' determination to avoid the hierophantic solemnity or self-lacerating irony of Symbolism.

TO SOMEONE GOING AWAY Originally dedicated to Gumilyov's inconstant fellow-Acmeist, Sergey Gorodetsky (1884–1967), who travelled to Italy in spring 1913. The 'Muse of Distant Wanderings', identified by some critics with the very essence of Gumilyov's work, had first appeared in his long poem 'The Discovery of America' (1910).

THE SEA AGAIN The last two lines draw on the Russian equivalent of 'the acceptable year of the Lord' from *Isaiah* 61.2 and *Luke* 4.19. This was something of a set-piece in the poetry of Gumilyov's older contemporaries. It was poignantly echoed in the latinized title of Akhmatova's *Anno Domini*, published in the immediate aftermath of his execution. The manuscript version of Gumilyov's poem had two extra stanzas, which amplified the theme of spiritual pilgrimage.

AFRICAN NIGHT Although the poem has generally been taken as an example of Gumilyov's aggressive imperialism, a different reading might emphasize the impartiality of his continuing fascination with competing spiritual traditions. Sidamo is in the south-west of Ethiopia.

THE ADVANCE Gumilyov's World War I poetry (see also 'The Sun of the Spirit' and 'Five-Foot Iambics') seems alien to the modern English sensibility shaped by Owen and Sassoon, but is close, for instance, to the tone of Rupert Brooke's 1914 'Sonnets' (compare the image of the 'national heart' here and in Brooke's 'The Soldier'). It draws on pastoral tradition, contemporary publicistic writing, and, in all probability, occult doctrine (e.g. Anthroposophy); but it is characterized above all by its high, religiously-oriented rhetoric. This is used to describe a fundamental dichotomy between body and spirit, utterly remote from the anti-German chauvinism typical of most Russian war poetry of the period. The event behind the present poem is the Russian advance on Vladislavov in Eastern Prussia (present-day Lithuania), which was Gumilyov's first experience of action in October 1914; but the prosaic reality of hungry troops, advancing in fear and blood through a heaven made hell, is contrasted and subordinated to the spiritual illumination of one imbued with the Word of God. And though the lyric persona is an ordinary soldier and one of many ('we'), this is obscured by his second hypostasis: a transfigured individual, 'victorious' over the flesh rather than the barely visible enemy, assured of the immortality of the spirit.

Stanza 1 – line 4 was suppressed by the military censors when the poem was published in 1915.

HEAVEN The opening of Gumilyov's very personal poem seems reminiscent in tone of the beginning of Byron's public satire, *The Vision of Judgement*: 'Saint Peter sat by the celestial gate; / His keys were rusty and the lock was dull.' For an unambiguously devout prototype of the poet's appeal for admittance to the celestial gate, see (again) Dante at the Gate of Purgatory (*Purgatory*, ix).

ISLAM Olga Nikolayevna Vysotskaya (1885–1966): actress in Vs. Meyerhold's experimental theatre troupe, mother of Gumilyov's illegitimate son, Orest Nikolayevich Vysotsky (Oct. 1913–1992). She subsequently lived in relative obscurity and died in Moldova. Gumilyov's son, after imprisonment in the late 1930s, active service in the war and a variety of jobs in the provinces, ended his career as a university lecturer in Kishinyov. With the advent of *glasnost*, he published some materials on his father's biography.

Gumilyov sent this poem by postcard to Vysotskaya during his long sea-voyage to Abyssinia, via Constantinople and Port Said, in April 1913. The 'cherry brandy' motif, elaborated in Russian through a series of extravagantly exotic rhymes, was echoed in Mandelstam's 1931 poem 'Sherry Brandy'. According to his widow: '"cherry brandy" – meaning "nonsense" – was an old joke', dating back to 'when he lived in Finland' (1912?). He evidently shared the joke with Gumilyov to engender this piece of Acmeist humour.

The Kaaba, said to have been erected by Abraham and Ishmael in the temple enclosure at Mecca, contains the black stone which supposedly fell from Paradise with Adam. On Damayanti, see note to 'Five-Foot Iambics'.

FABLE Teffi – pseudonym of N. A. Lokhvitskaya-Buchinskaya (1872–1952), at the time one of the leading contributors to the St Petersburg comic-satirical journal *Satirikon*. According to the Russian authority on Gumilyov, Yuri

Zobnin, this whimsical poem echoes elements of Teffi's book of verse, *Seven Fires*, and parodies the Gnostic cosmogony which fascinated the Symbolists. Akhmatova related it in part to a dream of Gumilyov's at Slepnyovo in 1912.

TREES This opening poem of *Bonfire* is typical of the collection in elaborating the concept of a magical nature which, according to the critic Raoul Eshelman, 'exists adjacent to man but remains ultimately inaccessible to him: it increases his eschatological yearning for salvation without actually allowing him to participate in transcendence.' The poet does not commune in the Romantic manner with the free, vegetable, animal and mineral world he observes, and cannot escape the restrictions of the human.

AUTUMN One of very few poems in which Gumilyov dispenses with rhyme and stanza – perhaps as part of the low-key emphasis on the uncultivated by-ways which often characterizes his and Akhmatova's depictions of their 'native' Tsarskoye Selo. This is in deliberate contrast to the 'Tsarskoye Selo' of poetic tradition, with the grand architecture of its imperial palace and formal avenues, and its imposing literary associations. 'Autumn', written in early 1917, echoes the description of rowans in Akhmatova's 1916 'Statue at Tsarskoye Selo'; but formal and lexical parallels also suggest a polemical re-working of the death-laden seasonal landscape of 'Autumn' by Zinaida Gippius (1869–1945), a Symbolist poet whose antipathy toward Gumilyov was mutual and long-established.

CHILDHOOD Another autobiographical evocation of Tsarskoye Selo – here, in March 1916, against the background of the war, from a perspective altered since 'The Advance' in the thematic direction of 'Trees' ('Childhood' was first entitled 'Grasses'). Alluded to in covert tribute to the forbidden Gumilyov both by G. Ivanov in 1921, and Akhmatova in 1940 ('The Willow', see Epilogue).

THE ICE FLOW With a detached humour, Gumilyov again introduces his personal distinction between human and natural worlds into the relatively common theme of Petersburg as a city of human incarceration. The opening lines echo Mandelstam's 'I am cold. The transparent spring' which was written in 1916, and borrowed the description of transparent spring greenery from Pushkin's *Eugene Onegin* (vii.i) to convey a vague apprehension of impending historical doom. Events had already moved on by the time of Gumilyov's poem, which is a response to the February Revolution of 1917.

I AND YOU Inscribed in the album of Yelena Karlovna Dubouchet (see on *Blue Star* below). In stanza 3, the imagery of knight, stars (again), and passive waiting implies that Symbolist poets are part of the bourgeois world 'foreign' to the poet. A recent Russian critic has noted acerbically of the fourth stanza that death in the presence of notary and doctor eluded the majority of Russia's major poets.

THE PEASANT The main subject of this poem, written in Petrograd in late March or April 1917, is the Siberian peasant Grigory Rasputin (b. 1872), the sinister imperial favourite supposedly possessed of supernatural powers, who was murdered by conspirators in 1916. His body was gruesomely exhumed and burned after the February Revolution of 1917. Some commentators have nevertheless seen Gumilyov's peasant as a composite image, also evocative of the folkloric 'robber-nightingale', of the 17th- and 18th-century rebels Stenka Razin and Pugachyov, and perhaps of the splendid peasant-poet Nikolay Klyuev (1887–1937). Many have remarked on Gumilyov's dispassionate presentation. To quote the poet Marina Tsvetayeva: 'What is there in this poem? Love? No. Hatred? No. Judgement? No. Justification? No. Fate. The Step of Fate'.

Stanza 8 – Kazan and St Isaac's are the two main cathedrals of St Petersburg-Petrograd.

THE WORKMAN The poem has often been read as prophetic of Gumilyov's execution (and, by Soviet critics, as a reflection of his bourgeois-imperialist antagonism toward the working class). But the 'foaming Dvina' (or Daugava), in present-day Latvia, marked the Russo-German front where he joined his regiment at Easter 1916 (his 30th birthday) and leaves no doubt that this is a poem inspired by World War I. Instead of a conventionally murderous 'enemy', however, the prosaic, remote, almost faceless workman seems the unwitting instrument of some ineluctable process of fate, accepted by the poet with a detachment and stoicism perhaps reminiscent of 'The Peasant'.

ON THE NORTH SEA Probably written in London in June 1917. An omitted manuscript stanza contained a rare expression of political sentiment in support of Britain and France.

COMFORT The poem contains several textual echoes of Gérard de Nerval's 'Les Cydalises'. It probably relates to the death of Masha Kuzmina-Karavayeva (see 'To a Girl').

DREAM Akhmatova maintained that this poem referred to her. It dates from early 1914. The image of the door in stanza 4 might conceivably be read in the light of her much later reminiscence: 'How many times did he tell me of the "golden door" that was to open for him in the depths of his wanderings, but when he returned [from Africa] in 1913 he admitted there was no "golden door". It was a terrible blow to him'.

EZBEKIE Another of Gumilyov's retrospective spiritual biographies from this period. The original, in splendidly controlled blank verse, derives some of its rhetorical authority from correspondences to Pushkin's late poem 'Again I visited. . .'.

The title refers to a garden in Cairo, which Gumilyov might have first visited during a month of obscure wanderings following his rejection by Akhmatova in summer 1907 (see note to 'Rejection', above; 'Ezbekie' dates from 1917). He was certainly in Cairo in autumn 1908, when he was thinking also of Vera Arens. His connection of Ezbekie with the wilful renunciation of suicide – which he had attempted on several occasions, ostensibly out of frustrated love – seems to correspond to reality. The consequent, stoical commitment to life on God's earth, whatever it may entail, is the very essence of his Acmeist morality. Akhmatova would accordingly allude obliquely to 'Ezbekie' in her late poetic masterpiece, *Poem Without a Hero*, to establish a contrast with the ignominious suicide of the poet Knyazev that is an important signal of the forbidden Gumilyov's status as her work's 'absent hero'.

Gumilyov passed through Cairo again in December 1909, and described the gardens with ironic self-detachment in a letter to Vera Shvarsalon, step-daughter of the Symbolist poet Vyacheslav Ivanov.

THE PORCELAIN PAVILION Like *Bonfire*, this small book was brought out through collaboration with Lozinsky in summer 1918, just before the terrible deprivations of the Civil War made publishing impossible. The poems are based on Western translations – principally *Le Livre de Jade* by Judith Gautier (daughter of Théophile Gautier, whose *Emaux et Camées* Gumilyov had admiringly translated before the war) – and are 'free variations' rather than precise renditions. Gumilyov's interest in Chinese (and Indo-Chinese) classical poetry, which several critics took to embody the spirit of Acmeism, is comparable with that of contemporaries such as Paul Claudel, or Ezra Pound and the Anglo-American Imagists. Gumilyov also appears to have discussed Chinese poetry with the British authority Arthur Waley, at the British Museum in London.

THE PORCELAIN PAVILION It is not impossible that this title-poem is part nostalgic evocation, from war-time London or Paris, of Tsarskoye Selo and its famous Chinese Park.

NATURE A comparable attitude to nature's imitation of man informs Mandelstam's Roman poems (c. 1914).

SUEZ CANAL From *Tent*, a series of 16 'African' poems, written under contract in 1918 as an experiment in 'geography in verse'. The full cycle was subsequently cut and reorganized by Gumilyov to intensify the impression of personal journey (or 'pilgrimage'), but should not be regarded as an accurate record of his own African travels. The poem is notable for its remoteness from the spirit of colonialism often attributed to Gumilyov.

THE EQUATORIAL FOREST The narrative perhaps reflects the enthusiasm for Rider Haggard and similar adventure tales sometimes apparent in Gumilyov's early poetry and prose. Stanza 10 – Gumilyov himself kept a quite detailed diary of his 1913 expedition to Abyssinia, partially preserved, and finally brought to light in the late 1980s, by his son Orest Vysotsky.

Stanza 20 – although the publication history of *Tent* is exceptionally complex, 'The Equatorial Forest' is essentially the last poem of the final authorized version. The concluding reference to the newspaper report therefore served to round off book as well as poem with the implication of 'return': to 'civilization' – or perhaps to the ravages of War-Communist Petrograd (cf. 'A Sentimental Journey').

FROM 'BLUE STAR' These poems date from Gumilyov's time in Paris, from July 1917–January 1918, in the service of the War Commissariat of the Provisional Government. They were inscribed in the album of his Parisian love, Yelena (Hélène) Karlovna Dubouchet, whom he referred to as his 'Blue Star'. Nothing is known of her, except that she was young, her father a French surgeon, her mother Russian (from an 'impoverished intellectual background') – and that she rejected Gumilyov to marry a rich American named Lovell, with whom she soon left to settle in Chicago. Despite the passionate tone of Gumilyov's poems (perhaps intensified by his awareness of Yelena Karlovna's engagement) it seems probable that he, too, had a second romantic involvement at the same time.

The lyrics – which were first published in Berlin two years after his death – are notably stylized, with many conventional images. They seem to draw on a tradition of courtly love, with its cult of noble feeling and refined expression, that dates back to the Provençal Troubadours. But though love itself is in this context of the highest spiritual value, one recent commentator has argued that the 'blue star' truly represents Lucifer, as a metaphor for demonic possession.

'FROM A WHOLE BOUQUET OF LILAC' The gift of the flower is one of the framing devices of the cycle: compare the last line of 'I said: "Do you want me..."'

'THE GOLDEN NIGHT WAS FLYING BY' The critic M. Iovanovich argues that the poem has a subtext in Mozart's *Magic Flute* – part of the Masonic symbolic system frequently apparent in *Blue Star* (a corollary of the poet's keen interest in his craftsmanship?). In general, the progress of the initiate is set against the sensual love of the woman, as a temptation liable to deflect him from his path. See also note to following poem.

'MONOTONOUS, MY DAYS FLASH PAST' Perhaps through the conventional association of nightingale with poet in the Persian poems of *The Pillar of Fire*, the striking image of the dead nightingale later became an Acmeist cipher for the executed Gumilyov. Mandelstam, for instance, asserted in his 'Notes on Chénier', that 'the whole of Romantic poetry, like a necklace of dead nightingales, refuses to give up its secrets.' The invocation of his murdered friend was all the stronger in that in the 1920s the name of Chénier, guillotined in 1794, itself became a coded allusion to Gumilyov.

Stanza 3 – Iovanovich finds here an allusion to the 'trial by air' which marks an advanced stage of Masonic initiation: the conjunction of the 'mountain heights' with the image of 'blind children' (ceremonially bandaged eyes?) may lend substance to his view. Other poems supposedly reflect trials by earth, water and fire – the former, for instance, in the 'blood-stained legs' of 'My heart had fought for so long'; trial by water, together with numerological symbolism, in 'A tenderly unprecedented joy'.

MEMORY Routinely quoted in biographical accounts of Gumilyov, but a clear example of the greatly increased complexity and profundity of his last collection. Stanza 1 – Gumilyov's opening image is possibly adapted from a poem by Bryusov; but it has several 'occult' parallels (e.g. in Freemasonry, Theosophy, Anthroposophy) and his idiosyncratic concept of a series of souls arguably develops the disjuncture between body and soul/spirit which he described in several earlier poems. Stanzas 3–4 – cf. 'Childhood' and 'Autumn'. Stanza 9: the uncertain distinction here between third and fourth 'souls' suggests an indebtedness to the Anthroposophical teachings of Rudolf Steiner. Stanza 10 – Gumilyov was twice awarded the George Cross for bravery in action, in December 1914 and July 1915; the physical 'tortures' recall 'The Advance'. Stanza 11 – see note to the Masonic imagery of 'Mediaeval'. Stanza 12 – several commentators have seen an echo of William Blake's 'Jerusalem' (which Gumilyov certainly knew); the shared source is the 'New Jerusalem' which comes 'down from God out of heaven' at the end of historical time in *Revelation*, 21. This 'holy city' is also prominent in Esoteric Freemasonry. Stanza 14 – the 'traveller' might be identified with Christ, and the lion and eagle with the Evangelists Mark and John. But it is possible to advance an alternative reading based on Nietzsche's anti-Christian, Zarathustrian 'Superman'; or to see an allusion to Dante's reunion with Beatrice at the summit of Mount Purgatory, where her face is hidden beneath a white veil and her retinue includes a gryphon (half-lion, half-eagle), symbolizing her two natures, human and divine: the 'understanding' which Dante here reaches after his long journey enables him to move on with her to Paradise (*Purgatory* xxix, xxxi). Or perhaps Gumilyov's traveller is Man as well as Christ (cf. the recurrent wanderer/pilgrim image) – the hitherto 'hidden' answer to the riddle of the compound beast, the Sphinx (see also *Ezekiel* 1).

THE FOREST Originally dedicated to Gumilyov's pupil, the young poet Irina Odoyevtseva (1895–1991) – subsequently the wife of Georgy Ivanov, and author of the most extensive available memoirs of Gumilyov. The dedication was removed after the critic Gollerbakh took the obvious physical resemblance of the poem's heroine to the red-haired Odoyevtseva as evidence of a relationship with Gumilyov. Gumilyov's outraged reaction was possibly disingenuous (cf. also 'No, nothing has changed'), but there followed an absurd literary scandal which was eventually resolved by a specially convened writers' court in spring 1921.

The theme of the woman's hair as a peopled forest may be one of several deep-level borrowings from Baudelaire typical of *The Pillar of Fire*: see his 'La Chevelure'.

THE WORD This highly rhetorical poem alludes to several Biblical texts, including *Genesis* 1.2 (lines 1–2; the face of God over the waters); *Joshua* 10.12–13 (line 3; the prophet's word halts the sun); *Joshua* 6 or *Proverbs* 11.11 (line 4; the destruction of the Walls of Jericho); and *John* 1.1 (stanza 5 – the Word as God) – the page of the Gospels often opened symbolically during Masonic rites. The possible subject of stanzas 3–4 is Pythagorean mysticism, much discussed by the Symbolists. Literary subtexts include an 1864 poem by Tyutchev on a Papal Bull condemning freedom of conscience, the opposition of which to Catholic authoritarianism doubtless assumed covert anti-Bolshevik resonance in 1919. The final, ostensibly illogical image of the bees in an empty hive (possibly suggested by Mandelstam's poem 'Dombey and Son', and reworked by him the following year in 'Take from my cupped hands for your delight/ a little sun and a little honey,/ as the bees of Persephone ordered us. . .') indicates, according to Eshelman, a breakdown of human community (and communication) – the result of man's failure to realize his spiritual potential through the imposition of material limitations.

The sense of a Divine Logos become elusive in the physical world now typifies Gumilyov's 'rational mysticism', and explains the fine balance of optimism (belief in the unconditional existence of an ordering Logos, as probable token of man's eventual release from spiritual impoverishment) and pessimism (its remoteness; the threat of intervening cataclysm) which informs the imperturbable acceptance of his own life and death. A secondary preoccupation – implicit here, and consequent upon the poet's particularly sharpened perceptions – is the status of his word (or 'Word'?) in relation to the will and authority of God, and the potential rôle (or otherwise) of the poet as modern- (or future-) day prophet and leader of mankind.

THE SOUL AND THE BODY Gumilyov draws here on an extraordinary range of spiritual traditions, including the Biblical; the classical (elements of Plato; the Elysian fields); Gnosticism (the myth of Sophia, reflected in the self-definition of 'the soul'); Nordic myth (Yggdrasil); and Hindu Brahmanism (the doctrine 'I am That'). To some extent, he may have borrowed in this from the example of Theosophy (or 'Ancient Wisdom') – the supposed 'synthesis and foundation of all philosophical teachings' propounded by Mme. Blavatsky and her followers. Blavatsky writes, for instance, of Yggdrasil, the Nordic 'tree of the universe', as the 'macrocosmic Tree' and 'Man himself', thus suggesting a basis for Gumilyov's concept of the fusion of inner self with universe; and she posits a 'universal' model of '7 planes and 49 sub-planes', redolent of Gumilyov's 'seven times seven universes'. But ultimately Gumilyov's latest treatment of the dichotomy of body and soul is as uniquely personal as the terms of his body's hymn to life. The result is not a definitive statement of belief, but a broad-ranging, speculative enigma, formulated within a precisely structured framework suggestive instead of logical clarity.

Stanza 1 – 'Have mercy, Lord, on marble souls' parodies a line from Blok: the original has 'nocturnal souls'. Section 2, stanza 1 – the transformation of gold to green is an alchemical image of degradation. It is perhaps also relevant that the colour green is associated with Venus, goddess of love. In contrast to the cold 'marble' soul's aversion to life and preoccupation with immortality, the body's intoxication with life brings it to the finality of death. For the imagery of intoxication, see 'The Drunk Dervish'. Section 3, stanza 1 – the constellation of the Great Bear is also known as 'The Plough' and as 'The Wagon', which in some esoteric traditions carries souls to heaven.

FIRST CANTO Probably addressed to Gumilyov's second wife, Anna Engelhardt (1895–1942). Although on one level the 'red, winged fire' is presumably a simple rooster, the wind so characteristic of *The Pillar of Fire* has been connected (among other possible occult sources) with the Stoic doctrine whereby wind is the bearer of the Divine Logos. Behind their subjective persona and tender intimacy, the two cantos prove consistent with the image structure and thematic preoccupations of preceding poems.

IMITATION OF THE PERSIAN Not known to have a specific source, but 'imitative' of the poetic conventions adopted by Sufi mysticism (see also 'The Drunk Dervish'; Gumilyov included 'Sufi poetry' in his lecture courses during 1919). This is a poetry of 'mystical eroticism' and 'mystical hedonism', in which love and wine are dominant metaphors for union with God: a striving toward the ultimate purpose of loss of self in the infinity of divine love. Hence, perhaps, the wry reversal of the last lines, where humiliation and self-abasement shift to a foretaste of triumph.

THE PERSIAN MINIATURE Gumilyov wrote from the trenches in January 1917 of his 'weakness' for exotic art, and his dream of amassing a splendid collection of Persian miniatures. This became possible, not at the Persian (or Mesopotamian) front to which he had hoped in vain to transfer, but in Paris later in the year – partly in the company of the artists Larionov and Goncharova. He was forced to leave his collection behind when ordered to set sail for Russia in April 1918.

The poem might be seen as a 'positive' rejoinder to the concluding stanzas of Baudelaire's 'Le Flacon' – though the modest, 'miniaturized' ambition otherwise goes scarcely beyond stoical resignation and a literal self-effacement. The critic Earl Sampson has suggested a thematic parallel with W. B.Yeats's 'Sailing to Byzantium'.

SIXTH SENSE Stanza 1 – 'beauty' and 'good' bear a powerful ethical load in Russian, and the Eucharistic connotations of bread and wine suggest the proximity of this outwardly very different, poignantly individualized poem to the 'mystical eroticism' used to articulate a comparable sense of physical and spiritual non-consummation in the traditionalized 'Imitation of the Persian'. A particular density of literary resonance, from Plato and Russian Sentimentalism to the young Mandelstam ('My turn will come,/ I feel the spread of the wing' in 'I hate the light. . .'), neatly reinforces the theme of 'age-long' frustration; while the 'mysterious desire' of the poet to transcend the 'limits' of nature – an 'impotence' sharpened by the meta-poetic paradox of the particular poem's birth/creation – returns us also, from a different temporal perspective (future rather than past) and stylistic idiom, to the underlying problematics of 'The Word'.

THE TRAM THAT LOST ITS WAY This most famous of Gumilyov's poems almost certainly dates from 29–30 December 1919, and originated in an incident when Gumilyov jumped aboard an empty tram in the deserted streets of early morning. Some commentators have attempted to correlate the journey Gumilyov describes to the real route of a Petrograd tram (a number 7), across the Trinity Bridge (hence 'three bridges'), past a market (Sytny Rynok: the vegetable market),with the Krechinsky mosque visible in the background (cf. the reference to Beirut), past Tuchkov Lane, where Gumilyov and Akhmatova had earlier rented a small flat, and finally past the zoological garden. The station selling tickets to the 'India of the Spirit' has been variously identified as a museum housing an exhibition of Indian art, the Nikolayevsky Station, and the Tsarskoye Selo Station. Clearly, however, the literal reading seems scarcely enough; and attempts have accordingly been made to interpret the tram's fantastic journey through time and space in the context of ideological systems ranging from Henri Bergson's philosophy to the Buddhist doctrine of transmigration (a 'tram-car of transmigration'). Perhaps most substantial and challenging in this respect has been Zobnin's argument that this is Gumilyov's re-writing of Dante's great journey, through the 'hell' of his own past to the posthumous reunion with Masha-Beatrice and eventual accession to the heavenly garden. The poem has also been taken as a re-working of Rimbaud's 'Le Bâteau ivre'; and illuminatingly described in the extensive context of the 'tram' theme in contemporary Russian poetry (Roman Timenchik). Echoes of the tram journey are to be found in two of the century's most important Russian novels: Mikhail Bulgakov's *Master and Margarita*, and at the hero's death in Boris Pasternak's *Doctor Zhivago*.

Stanzas 1–3 – Zobnin sees in the tram's approach a modern-day version of Dante losing his way in the dark wood in the middle of life's journey. There are several probable allusions to earlier works by Gumilyov, while the 'driver' echoes the epithet used by Dante of Virgil. Stanza 4 – the Neva, Nile and Seine all have clear relevance to stages in Gumilyov's own biography. Stanza 6 – the India of the Spirit might also allude to a long early poem by Gumilyov, 'The Northern Rajah', which placed the illusory 'kingdom' of art above reality; an allusion, then, to early, Symbolist-oriented delusion. Stanza 9 – Akhmatova recognized this as the Shukhardin house where she had lived as a girl in Tsarskoye Selo; but the three windows have also been interpreted as a religious allegory. Stanza 10 – 'where now are your body and voice' is a clear allusion to Akhmatova (who had virtually ceased writing at this time): see her 'Dying, I am exhausted with thoughts of immortality', whose last lines are 'People will come and bury/my body and my voice.' But the date of the poem's composition is the exact anniversary of Masha Kuzmina-Karavayeva's death in 1911 (see 'To A Girl'). It therefore seems probable that this 'Russian Beatrice' is a composite figure from the poet's own life. Stanza 11 – an allusion to Pushkin's story *The Captain's Daughter* has usually been detected here; but a more probable source is an incident in the life (and verse) of the 18th-century poet Gavriil Derzhavin, torn between loyalty to his friends and sovereign, and care for his dying wife. Gumilyov enlisted in the regiment of the Empress Alexandra – and met her personally in military hospital in Tsarskoye Selo. By the time his service had ended, of course, he had lost Akhmatova. Stanza 12 – a possible reference to Dante's Heaven. Stanza 13 – the rider is Falconet's statue of Peter the Great, symbol of autocracy and Russian historical destiny, celebrated (and demonized) in Pushkin's masterpiece *The Bronze Horseman*. Stanza 14 – St Isaac's Cathedral became a focus for Orthodox opposition to Bolshevism at this time. A clandestine requiem had been celebrated there for another Nikolay – the murdered Tsar, Nikolay II.

OLGA Probably addressed to the actress Olga Arbenina (1899–1980; schoolfriend of Gumilyov's second wife, object of Mandelstam's as well as Gumilyov's attentions during 1920), although another Olga, the poet and translator Olga Mochalova (1898–1981) laid claim to the same honour.

Proceeding from the etymology of the Christian name Olga from Old Norse (H)elga (= Holy – an evident paradox in the subsequent pagan context of Norse 'Valhalla' and 'Valkyries'), the poem is a meditation on the combined brutality and spirituality of Russian history – and hence the nature of 'Russianness', and the poet's self – against the background of the legendary descent of Russian princes from the Varangian (Scandinavian) prince, Ryurik. The lineage was claimed till the fall of the dynasty of the Romanovs. Stanza 2 – the Kievan Princess Olga (d. 969) was Russia's first Christian ruler, baptized c. 957. In 945 she had taken vengeance on the West Slav tribe of the Drevlyane for the murder of her husband Igor by burning their leaders alive in a bath-house. Drevlyane is etymologically related to the word for 'ancient'. Stanzas 3 and 7 – Kiev, 'cradle of the Russian State', rose to prosperity because of its position on the trade route from the Varangians to the Byzantine Greeks. Olga ruled in Kiev while her son Svyatoslav campaigned 'beyond the seas'; according to the Russian *Primary Chronicle*, his skull was used as a drinking vessel by the Pechenegs who killed him in ambush.

WITH THE GYPSIES Probably dedicated to the gypsy singer Nina Shishkina, with whom Gumilyov was rumoured to have had an affair.

It is scarcely surprising that correspondences can be discerned to Blok's famous 'gypsy' and 'restaurant' poems, as well as to Lermontov's 'Feast of Asmodeus'; but no less significant are parallels to Gumilyov's own early work: his undistinguished poem 'At the Feast', or his connection of music with the devil in his story 'The Stradivarius Violin' and related texts. According to the young scholar T. S. Zorina, this initiates an excursion into his own Symbolist past, and backward, via the Baudelairean connection of gypsies with the infernal or nether world, from the personal unconscious to the mythical past of mankind. (There are possible references to the dance of Shiva and the rites of Dionysus – the torn-out heart; tiger and bull as Dionysian attributes – as well as to the 'Creator' and 'Christian' demonology). From yet another, highly distinctive angle, the confrontation with the primitive central to such 'neighbouring' pieces as 'Olga' and 'The Leopard' is thus treated again in this dense, enigmatic poem.

Stanza 1 – Gumilyov himself transferred to the Hussars in 1916, but the uniform was no longer red. An initial indication, then, of the journey backward through time.

THE DRUNK DERVISH A consummately skilful condensation of a longer lyric by the Sufi poet Nasir-i-Khusraw (b. 1003/4). In Sufism, God is pure essence; and all that is not God, including the entire phenomenal world, exists only in so far as it is imbued by that essence, of which it is the mere reflection or shadow. 'Wine' symbolizes mystical intoxication with divine love, and the dervish is one who has accepted poverty to devote himself entirely to the goal of self-abnegating union with the Godhead. But in a modern Russian context this allegorical meaning is considerably complicated by a range of other implications. Not least of these is the significance of Gumilyov's dervish as poet, describing the enigma of inspiration, drawing in part on the authority of his dead friends.

Akhmatova used the poem's refrain as an epitaph for Gumilyov, taking it as epigraph to the section 'Voice of Memory' from her 1922 book *Anno Domini*.

THE LEOPARD Gumilyov had kept a leopard skin which he brought back from Abyssinia in his study at Tsarskoye Selo. He had also published a prose sketch describing how he had hunted a leopard (probably in 1910) and, having shot it, had been overcome by a momentary horror: 'I felt that all the beasts of Africa had lain down around me, and were awaiting their moment to kill me, painfully and shamefully'. Stanza 6 – the line 'my brother, my enemy' was later adapted by Mandelstam in his 1922 poem 'The Age'. Stanza 10 – Danakil: an Ethiopian tribe (cf. Gumilyov's poem 'Abyssinia').

THE MASTER CRAFTSMEN'S PRAYER Another poem with overtly Masonic connotations; probably written in response to the initial reception of Akhmatova's *Plantain* (1921) and as a polemical reiteration of Gumilyov's own ideal of the self-possessed craftsman – concentrated in purpose, refusing to overreach himself. It seems to echo the 'disciples' malicious mockery' from Akhmatova's 1915 poem 'For us the freshness of words'; and to align itself also with the last couplet of Pushkin's famous version of the Horatian 'Exegi monumentum' theme.

BIRD-GIRL Broceliande is the legendary land – or forest – where Vivien bewitched and for ever imprisoned Merlin. It is usually identified with the Forest of Paimpont in Brittany, site also of the 'Valley of No Return', domain of Morgan le Fay. Like 'The Forest', the poem reflects Gumilyov's interest in both Celtic folklore and Arthurian Romance (he had long been familiar with Chrétien de Troyes and other mediaeval texts, and probably also knew Tennyson's *Idylls of the King*). The plot is nevertheless his own. Sergey Makovsky (see 'I Believed, I Thought') saw the Bird-Girl as Masha Kuzmina-Karavayeva, and this poetic 'cryptogram in Maeterlinckian-Romantic vein' as the very essence of Gumilyov's work: 'The Bird-Girl is his inspiration, his spiritual mother, and simultaneously the girl to whom his soul aspires, he, the "herdsman", who does not yet know his Muse because . . . he is not yet "born" as prescient poet, but still sings carefree "joyous songs". Not knowing what he does, he kills her with a kiss. His fate brings no joy, and the bird he has killed will call to him from another, transformed world. This is Gumilyov's true Muse.'

Comparison with Blok's poem 'The Artist' lends further substance to a reading in terms of poetic creation.

MY READERS Chronologically the last poem of *The Pillar of Fire* – almost certainly written (and inserted at the last minute) in response to Alexander Blok's jaundiced attack on the 'soullessness' of Gumilyov and Acmeism in his essay 'Without Divinity, Without Inspiration' (late April 1921: Blok was already in fact seriously ill, and died on 7 August). Hence, it would seem, the element of anti-aesthetic bravado, emphasized (despite a probably inadvertent resemblance to Mikhail Kuzmin's poem 'My Ancestors') by the form of the original – Gumilyov's only excursion into unrhymed free verse. Stanza 1 – the 'old vagabond' was apparently familiar to friends from Gumilyov's oral reminiscences; the daring lieutenant was the young poet Sergey Kolbasyev (1899–1938?), whom Gumilyov met on a trip to the Crimea in July 1921; the assassin of the German Ambassador to Russia was Yakov Blyumkin (1898–1929), vividly described in Nadezhda Mandelstam's memoir, *Hope Against Hope*. Stanza 2 – the first line is a polemical restatement of the ending of Blok's 'Autumn Freedom'. Stanza 3 – 'neurasthenia' is intended as the professional disease of self-absorbed Symbolists, and the polysemantic conjecture over a 'half-empty' egg as a parody of their futile metaphysical concerns. The line 'not to fear and to do what has to be done' has been read as a call to anti-Bolshevik insurgency. The closing sentiments are of course typical of the mature Gumilyov; the final encounter with death, so fundamental to *The Pillar of Fire*, might be compared with 'Memory', 'The Tram that Lost its Way', 'The Persian Miniature', 'The Leopard', etc.

STAR TERROR Stanza 2 – Zend: an Iranian tribe. 'Woe! Woe!...': this powerful refrain, related to *Isaiah* 24.17 ('Fear and the pit, and the snare are upon thee, O inhabitant of earth') on the authority of Akhmatova and Mandelstam's widow, occurs also in *Jeremiah* 48.43, and is partially reiterated in another of Gumilyov's persistent sources, *Revelation* (8.13). The cumulative contexts underscore the potential topical relevance to a time of cataclysmic political upheaval.

On Gumilyov and the stars, see note to the early poem 'In the Heavens'; here, possibly, compare the long meditative passage on the stars in Lermontov's tale 'The Fatalist'. A different framework for interpreting the poem is offered by the literary critic Harold Bloom's etymological observation on the word 'influence', in 'its root meaning of "inflow", and its prime meaning of an emanation or force coming in upon mankind from the stars'. This is a prelude to Bloom's disquisition on the 'anxiety' and even 'terror' of creative influence, necessarily entailing the broader issues of intellectual heresy and revisionism, and the nature of 'enslavement to another's system'.

MY HOUR One of several free-stanzaic meditations in nocturnal Petrograd, this one from 1919. Stanza 2 – 'maned nightmare' may be an etymologically inspired reification of the demon Maera; the second half of the stanza possibly evokes the dazzling seduction of Tamara in Lermontov's narrative poem *The Demon*. Stanza 3 – the imagery of nocturnal silence was perhaps echoed, in covert tribute to the dead husband, in Akhmatova's graphic description of the onset of the poetic impulse in her 1936 poem 'Creation'. The image of the owl was taken up in Mandelstam's 'Slate Ode'. Stanza 4 – 'the uniqueness of a single earthly stem' – perhaps another reflection of the late Gumilyov's approximation to the mysticism of Blake ('To see a World in a Grain of Sand / And a Heaven in a Wild Flower. . .' etc.).

'THE WHITE WILLOW . . .' Akhmatova believed that the poem was addressed to Olga Arbenina, and detected an echo of Baudelaire's 'Le Voyage' in the final stanza.

A SENTIMENTAL JOURNEY Apparently sent to Olga Arbenina in a letter of March 1920; but another variant is dated 1918, revealing Gumilyov's perhaps questionable practice of making occasional adjustments in order to dedicate the same poem to different women.

Section 2 – compare Gumilyov's first-hand impressions in his letter from Cairo to Vera Shvarsalon in 1909 (see note to 'Ezbekie'): 'I got off the boat at Piraeus, visited the Acropolis, and prayed to Pallas Athene before her temple. I realized that she is alive as in the times of Odysseus, and think of her with such joy.' He had also made brief visits to Greece via 'Stambul' in 1908, and possibly 1907. Section 3 – 'An evil night in Petersburg': a deliberate anachronism, perhaps in part to highlight the contrast between Civil War Petrograd and the Petersburg of Pushkin, who depicted himself, pen in hand, in the benevolent, white night of the city in the 'Introduction' to his masterpiece *The Bronze Horseman*. At the same time, this closing invocation of immediate reality conveys with a new force the contrast between journey and stifling stasis implicit in many early poems of Gumilyov.

'THE POET IS LAZY. . .' As in so much of his love poetry, Gumilyov seeks to express his individuality not merely through traditional tropes and classical imagery, but also by aligning himself with the experience of Russian predecessors. Here he recalls his early mentor, Valery Bryusov, in his formulation of the subordination of love to poetry; and Pushkin in his rendition of the poet's dramatic transfiguration from 'laziness' to god-like inspiration.

'YOU AND I ARE BOUND. . .' Line 8 – an ironic reversal of Hamlet's 'I could be bounded in a nutshell, / And count myself a king of infinite space'?

'THE HEART IS MORE AFLAME. . .' The authoritative commentator Roman Timenchik sees the poem – and particularly Gumilyov's 'Venutian astro-linguistics' – as part-experiment, part-parody in the vein of such Russian avant-garde movements as Ego- and Cubo-Futurism and Scientism (with an evident gesture towards Rimbaud's 'Voyelles'). But it also contains a statement on the immortality of the poet-pilgrim which acquired the resonance of an epitaph for some of his followers.

'I PLAYED A JOKE ON MYSELF' Probably dedicated to the young poet Nina Berberova (1901–1993), to whom Gumilyov presented the poem in manuscript on 1 August 1921 – two days before his arrest. Berberova became the common-law wife of the major poet V. F. Khodasevich (1886–1939), with whom she emigrated in 1922; she recalled her brief encounter with Gumilyov in her literary autobiography, *The Italics are Mine* (1969). The white garment of stanza 2 apparently describes her white dress; the crystal spheres are associated with poetic creation as well as divination, thanks to the famous ending of Pushkin's *Eugene Onegin*.

'I CAME BACK' One of Gumilyov's last poems, all the more poignant for its promise of a new poetic idiom.

Instead of an Epilogue
Some poems of Anna Akhmatova
to or about Nikolay Gumilyov

'HE LOVED THREE THINGS. . .'

He loved three things in this world:
evensong, white peacocks
and faded maps of America.
He didn't like crying children,
he didn't like raspberry jam with his tea —
and womanish hysterics.
. . . And I was his wife.

1911

'I WAS RETURNING HOME FROM SCHOOL'

I was returning home from school
with my pencil box and books in my satchel.
Surely these lime trees have not forgotten
our meeting, my happy boy.
Only the grey cygnet changed
when he became the proud swan.
Sorrow lay on my life with an eternal ray
and my own voice is muted.

1912 *Tsarskoye Selo*

'I WILL LEAVE YOUR WHITE HOUSE...'

I will leave your white house and quiet garden.
May your life be empty and bright.
I will glorify you, you in my poems,
as no woman ever could.
Remember your dear friend
in the heaven created by you for her eyes;
I trade in rarest goods —
I sell your love and tenderness.

1913

LULLABY

'Far away in a huge forest,
by the blue rivers,
lived a poor woodsman with his children
in a dark hut.

The youngest son was a tiny child.'
Hush now, my baby,
sleep my quiet one, sleep my little boy —
I am a bad mother.

News seldom gets through to our house
but we did hear that
your father got
the little white cross.

There were hard times and there will be again,
no end to the hard times —
let Saint George protect
your father.

c. 1915

'THAT AUGUST. . .'

That August, like a yellow flame
bursting through the smoke,
that August rose above us
like a fiery seraph.

Into the city of sadness and anger,
from the quiet Karelian land,
we two – the warrior and the maiden –
entered on a chill morning.

What had happened to our capital,
who had brought down the sun to earth?
The black eagle on the standard
seemed to be a bird flying.

The city of fine displays
was like a savage camp,
the flashing of lances and bayonets
blinded the eyes of passers-by.

The grey cannons thundered
on the reverberating Troitsky bridge
and the lime trees were still green
in the mysterious Summer Garden.

My brother said to me:
'My days of glory have begun,
now you alone must preserve
our sadness and joy.'

It was as though he'd left
the keys of his manor to the housekeeper,
and the east wind glorified
the feather-grass of the steppe by the Volga.

1915

'TERROR, RUMMAGING THROUGH THINGS IN THE DARK'

Terror, rummaging through things in the dark,
aims a moonbeam at an axe.
A sinister thud from behind the wall —
what's there, rats, a ghost, or a thief?

It splashes like water in the claustrophobic kitchen,
counts the shaky floorboards,
it flashes past the attic window
with a glossy, black beard,

then silence. How evil and crafty is terror,
it hid the matches and blew out the candle.
I'd rather the gleam of the rifle
barrels aimed at my breast,

rather lie down on the unpainted scaffold
on the green square
and for my life blood to flow out
to the crowd's groans and screams of joy.

I press the smooth crucifix to my breast:
O God bring peace back to me.
That sweet smell of decay wafts
in a swoon from the cool sheet.

25 or 27–28 August 1921 *Tsarskoye Selo*

'THE CRIED-OUT AUTUMN...'

The cried-out autumn, like a widow
wearing black, shrouds all hearts...
Running through her husband's words
she cannot stop sobbing.
It will be like this until the quietest snow
takes pity on the exhausted mourner...
The oblivion of pain and the oblivion of bliss:
to give up one's life for this is no small thing.

15 September 1921 *Tsarskoye Selo*

INCANTATION

From the prison gates,
from the marshes beyond the Okhta,
by an untrod path,
by the unscythed meadow,
through the cordon of night,
under the Easter peal,
uninvited,
not my fiancé,
come to me for supper.

15 April 1936

WILLOW

And a decrepit bunch of trees — PUSHKIN

I grew in patterned silence
in the cool nursery of the century.
Man's voice held no sweetness for me
but I understood the wind.
I loved the burdocks and nettles
but above all the silver willow.
Thankful it lived with me
all its life, weeping branches
fanning sleeplessness with dreams.
Strange — I outlived it.
Now a stump sticks up there, other willows
say something in strange voices
under our — under those — heavens.
I am silent. . . as though my brother were dead.

18 January 1940

Notes to Akhmatova poems

BY MICHAEL BASKER

'I was returning home from school', 'That August. . .' and 'The cried-out autumn' have been translated by Richard McKane for this edition. The remaining six poems are from his *Anna Akhmatova: Selected Poems* (Bloodaxe Books, 1989).

'HE LOVED THREE THINGS. . .' It is as typical of Akhmatova as of Gumilyov that this deceptively simple portrait-poem generates meaning partly through allusion to other texts. Gumilyov's enthusiasm for 'faded maps of America' had found recent literary expression in the long poem 'The Discovery of America' – which he completed in October 1910, during the sea-voyage to Africa which began his six-month absence from Akhmatova less than half a year into their marriage. He had posted it home, and it would have been fresh in Akhmatova's mind as she was writing this (in Kiev with her mother). But the love of 'faded maps' she attributes to the husband in her poem might also have been intended as an ironic contrast to the more authentically vigorous hero of Gumilyov's poem of the year before, 'Captains I': 'The captain's breast is splashed not with dust/of lost charts, but with sea-salt'. A similarly ironic effect is achieved through the dislike of 'crying children' (line 4). This is made pointedly reprehensible by implicit contrast with lines from 'The Anguish of Recollection' by Innokenty Annensky (1855–1909) – the Tsarskoye Selo poet over whom Akhmatova was then enthusing, and one-time headmaster, now posthumously revered model, of Gumilyov: 'I like children in the house,/And when they cry at night'.

It scarcely needs adding that Akhmatova's wry poem is a model of laconic restraint, effective precisely for its distanced avoidance of the hysterical outpouring which the husband so dislikes (Gumilyov was to deal most forthrightly with the subject of 'womanish hysterics' the following spring, in 'From a Dragon's Lair'). Her simple use of the past tense to describe the marriage – as early as 1910 – seems eloquently crushing. Unusually, but perhaps unsurprisingly given its intimate content, she did not republish this piece after its first appearance in print in 1912.

'I WAS RETURNING HOME FROM SCHOOL' The opening evocation of the meeting between Akhmatova and Gumilyov as schoolchildren in

Tsarskoye Selo has its counterpart in the 'tender' conclusion of Gumilyov's 'Modernity', written the previous year (1911). The transformation of cygnet to swan might obviously recall the 'Tale of the Ugly Duckling': appropriately enough, Andersen had been one of Gumilyov's favourite childhood authors. But the swan, like the lime trees, was also a recurrent signal of Tsarskoye Selo – and more specifically of its poets. In another poem of 1911, 'To the Memory of Annensky', Gumilyov had likened the latter to the 'last swan of Tsarskoye Selo', not only in order to suggest a continuity between Annensky and the tradition of Pushkin and Zhukovsky, but also, paradoxically, to assert his own accession to their illustrious lineage. In this context, Akhmatova's reference to cygnet-become-swan can be interpreted as reinforcing Gumilyov's polemical message, implying his sudden evolution from Symbolist 'boy' to majestic Acmeist maturity. And although lines 7–8 ostensibly describe the suppression of her own poetry as a result, her 'muted voice' echoes that of another major 19th-century poet, Yevgeny Baratynsky (1800–44), thereby subtly allying her poetry also to the classical heritage so crucial to Acmeism: personal sorrow is thus entirely compatible with Acmeist art.

'I WILL LEAVE YOUR WHITE HOUSE. . .' Akhmatova herself afterwards privately affirmed that this related to Gumilyov. In contrast to the preceding poem, it is the woman poet who here takes the active lead. But the split between private and artistic lives (implicit, perhaps, in Gorenko-Gumilyova's assumption of the pen-name 'Akhmatova'), and the sense that the former is ultimately subordinate to the latter, typifies the outlook of both poets, and must have played a significant part in their relationship. In Akhmatova, however, the attendant sense of personal guilt is more developed, as too is their shared preoccupation with the poet's power to bestow fame.

LULLABY Stanza 1 – the setting possibly echoes that of an early poem by Gumilyov, 'The Princess'. The diction, however, is borrowed from the Russian folk tradition, and the cadences of the original from Lermontov's famous 'Cossack Lullaby'. Stanza 2 – in an unpublished version of the 1920s, the poem bore a dedication to Akhmatova's son, Lev Gumilyov, who was to a large extent brought up by his paternal grandmother. Stanza 3 – the reference is to the award of the Cross of St George, for which Gumilyov was commended in December 1914. He received a second decoration in December 1915, for his part in a successful counter-attack against the Austrians that July. Stanza 4 – St George, whose name is given in the original in its folk-form Yegory, was the patron saint of the Russian soldier.

'THAT AUGUST. . .' Stanza 1 – the reference is to the first days of war, in August 1914, while the imagery of angels and smoke echoes Gumilyov's 1913 poem 'Old Manor Houses'. In August 1939, when Akhmatova learned that Lev Gumilyov was to be sent to a camp in the north, she would tell her friend Lydia Chukovskaya that August had always been a 'month of terror' for her. It was the month of Gumilyov's death and of the campaign of vilification which Stalin's 'cultural spokesman' A. A. Zhdanov would launch against her in 1946. Stanza 2 – Gumilyov and Akhmatova returned together to Petersburg-Petrograd on 2 August – not in fact from Karelia, but from the family home at Slepnyovo, to the south-east, where Gumilyov had gone to say his farewells before joining up. But when war broke out in July, Gumilyov had been (alone) on the borders of Karelia: at Terioki on the Gulf of Finland, where he had planned to spend the summer. According to Akhmatova's most recent editor, N. V. Korolyova, the iconic image of warrior and maiden may reflect the words of Akhmatova's father as he lay dying the following August, 1915. Stanza 3 – compare Gumilyov's subsequent description of the dramatic transformation of the capital in 'The Peasant'. Stanza 4 – the city's fine military displays are memorably described in the Introduction to Pushkin's *The Bronze Horseman*. Stanza 6 – it seems characteristic of their 'poetic' relationship that Gumilyov and Akhmatova repeatedly referred to each other in their verse as brother and sister. Like the religious imagery of stanza 1, the warrior's words here might be compared to the ending of Gumilyov's 'Five-Foot Iambics'. But it should also be borne in mind that Akhmatova's younger brother, Viktor, was sent off at this time to serve in the Black Sea Fleet. Stanza 7 – the shift 'eastwards' from the westernized capital is in keeping with the 'Russian' element of the previous poem.

'TERROR, RUMMAGING THROUGH THINGS IN THE DARK' Akhmatova provided two different dates for this poem. In either case, as often in her mature work, the dateline is a vital component of meaning. She later believed Gumilyov was shot on 25 August 1921; but she did not learn of his death until 1 September – from a newspaper pinned to the wall of the Tsarskoye Selo station which had played such a part in their lives.

Stanzas 1–2 – these images of intangible domestic menace (with strong peasant coloration – the axe and the black beard) were to be taken up in several other poems, which constitute something of a 'cycle of fear' inspired by Gumilyov's death (see especially 'A monstrous rumour roams over the city'). 'Terror, rummaging. . .' also provided a subtext for Mandelstam's response to Gumilyov's execution:

> I washed in the courtyard at night –
> the sky shone with coarse stars.
> Beam of a star, like salt on an axe,
> the full barrel freezing.

The gates are locked,
and the world quite honestly is so strict:
I doubt if one could ever find a base
of fresh canvas as pure as truth.

Like salt a star thaws in the barrel,
and the ice-cold water is blacker,
death purer, trouble more bitter,
and the world more honest, more terrible.

1921   *Tr. Richard McKane*

Stanza 4 – as the scene shifts from the claustrophobic private domain to unrealized yearning for drastic public resolution, the combination of green, blood and scaffold seems to evoke Gumilyov's 'The Tram that Lost its Way', and perhaps also his presentiment of death in 'Childhood'. Stanza 5 – the closing image was written under Akhmatova's impressions of the requiem mass for Alexander Blok, which she attended in his flat on 8 August 1921. It was at Blok's funeral two days later that she learned of Gumilyov's arrest. The premature deaths in the same August (Blok was 40) of Petrograd's two most prominent poets are thus intertwined in the final stanza; and the haunted heroine is left, alive and alone, to contemplate her own fate. As the scholar Omry Ronen has written: 'One of Akhmatova's pervasive themes, the theme of agonizing expectation of death, reached its turning point in this poem, as history began to realize the poet's earlier lyrical metaphors.'

'THE CRIED-OUT AUTUMN. . .' Akhmatova's first poem since learning of Gumilyov's death. As Roman Timenchik has shown, its imagery derives in part from *Red-Nose Frost*, Nekrasov's long poem on the sufferings of a peasant woman, which Akhmatova remembered from childhood. Her typically impersonal, third-person objectification and generalization of personal grief is a consistent development of her approach in 'He loved three things'.

Line 3 – it is no coincidence that the verb here (*perebirat'*) was also used in response to the same event in line 1 of the previous poem. Line 7 – the theme of oblivion (forgetting) should be set against Akhmatova's conviction that her poetry was based on recollection and, increasingly from this point, that it was a commemorative act. Oblivion thus becomes tantamount to an agonizing abdication of moral and artistic responsibility.

INCANTATION First published in the 1960s over the deliberately misleading date '1935' – intended to conceal from the Soviet censorship that the poem was written on what would have been Gumilyov's fiftieth birthday.

(Following the change from the Julian to the Gregorian or Western calendar in 1918, 'old style' 3 April became 15 April.) Also for reasons of censorship, 'tall' was substituted for 'prison' in line 1. Motifs of sorcery and necromancy are common in Akhmatova's later verse. This poem appears to draw both on the Russian (pagan) folk ritual of offering food to dead relatives at Easter-time, and, with a ghoulish twist, on the texts of invocations used by unmarried girls to divine the identity of a future husband.

Line 2 – the marshes can be identified as the spot near the village of Berngardovka outside Petersburg-Petrograd, by now renamed Leningrad, where Akhmatova believed Gumilyov had been shot. (It has recently been established that the Tagantsev executions were in fact carried out on the site of the Rzhevsk artillery range, closer to the city.) Lines 3–5 – the untrodden and forbidden paths are presumably those by which the dead may return. Line 4 – 'by the unscythed meadow' (*lugom nekoshennym* in Russian) may also constitute a near-anagrammatic invocation of 'Nik. Gumilyov' (discovered by the scholar Mikhail Meilakh). Line 6 – April was also the month of the poets' wedding: they were married immediately after Easter, on 25 April 1910. Lines 7–9 – in addition to folk motifs, there may be an inversion here of the Don Juan legend which Akhmatova used repeatedly from this time to allude to Gumilyov.

WILLOW The epigraph is from Pushkin's poem 'Tsarskoye Selo'. The link with the forbidden Gumilyov is indicated by the images of the wild child's affinity with wind and burdock (compare his 'Childhood', 'Autumn', and 'Memory'); and may be reinforced by the closing reference to the dead brother (see note on 'That August. . .'). But this last line has a counterpart also in Tyutchev; and the poem is replete with echoes of other 'voices' become strange or 'alien' in the era into which Akhmatova alone has survived: Lermontov, Byron, Dante, and even the Psalms (Psalm 137). The 'silver willow' is undoubtedly in part a metaphor for the 'Silver Age'; and its Tsarskoye Selo representatives – Akhmatova, Gumilyov and Annensky – are linked by a further complex of allusions, beginning with the epigraph, to the era of Pushkin and Zhukovsky. In the Soviet Union in January 1940, the last lone voice seemed to be facing a descent into total silence. As it turned out, however, this would be Akhmatova's most productive year since 1921 and 'Willow' marked the beginning of a remarkable period of creativity, which would culminate that December in the impetus for her masterpiece *Poem Without a Hero*. Its absent hero, deeply concealed, is Gumilyov.

About Survivors' Poetry

Survivors' Poetry is an innovative national literature and performance organization dedicated to promoting poetry by survivors of mental distress through workshops, performances, readings, publishing, networking and training. It was founded in 1991 by four poets with first-hand experience of the mental health system and is managed entirely by survivors.

A survivor may be defined as a person with a current or past experience of psychiatric hospitals, a recipient of ECT, tranquillizers or other medication, a user of counselling services, a survivor of sexual abuse, child abuse, and any other person who has empathy with the experience of survivors.

In spite of the prevalence of mental distress – affecting one in four people at any one time – there are still strong prejudices and misconceptions in society at large. Survivors' Poetry works to reduce this prejudice by offering survivors opportunities to give creative voice to their experience through performance and publishing. We support the formation of a nationwide network of survivors' writing groups and work in partnership with local and national arts, mental health, community and disability organizations.

No one knows why at times of heightened emotion many people are compelled to write poetry, but often, out of the pain of experience, there come poems that are testimony to the transcending power of the imagination; an expression which has moved from the purely personal to something which has universal significance – a work of art.

Some publications from Survivors' Poetry Press

Fresher than Green, Brighter than Orange
An anthology of poetry by Irish women living in London in 1999
Edited by Eamer O'Keeffe & Lisa Boardman

Under the Asylum Tree
An illustrated anthology of poetry
Edited by Jenny Ford, Colin Hambrook & Hilary Porter

From Dark to Light
An illustrated anthology of poetry
Edited by Frank Bangay, Joe Bidder & Hilary Porter

For information please write to

Survivors' Poetry
Diorama Arts Centre
34 Osnaburgh Street
London NW1 3ND